S. Hrg. 113–500

DELIVERING BETTER HEALTH CARE VALUE TO CONSUMERS: THE FIRST THREE YEARS OF THE MEDICAL LOSS RATIO

HEARING

BEFORE THE

COMMITTEE ON COMMERCE, SCIENCE, AND TRANSPORTATION UNITED STATES SENATE

ONE HUNDRED THIRTEENTH CONGRESS

SECOND SESSION

MAY 21, 2014

Printed for the use of the Committee on Commerce, Science, and Transportation

U.S. GOVERNMENT PRINTING OFFICE

91–652 PDF   WASHINGTON : 2014

For sale by the Superintendent of Documents, U.S. Government Printing Office
Internet: bookstore.gpo.gov   Phone: toll free (866) 512–1800; DC area (202) 512–1800
Fax: (202) 512–2104   Mail: Stop IDCC, Washington, DC 20402–0001

CONTENTS

DELIVERING BETTER HEALTH CARE VALUE TO CONSUMERS: THE FIRST THREE YEARS OF THE MEDICAL LOSS RATIO

WEDNESDAY, MAY 21, 2014

U.S. SENATE,
COMMITTEE ON COMMERCE, SCIENCE, AND TRANSPORTATION,
Washington, DC.

The Committee met, pursuant to notice, at 2:53 p.m. in room SD–253, Russell Senate Office Building, Hon. John D. Rockefeller IV, presiding.

OPENING STATEMENT OF HON. JOHN D. ROCKEFELLER IV, U.S. SENATOR FROM WEST VIRGINIA

The CHAIRMAN. Welcome, all. This committee hearing comes to order. So today, and the Ranking Member does not have to sort of hear this statement, but I will just give it. He can put plugs in his ears. Today's hearing is about an Obama success story.

Senator THUNE. Go ahead. Proceed.

The CHAIRMAN. It is about a consumer protection provision in the law, which is already existing in one way or another in 34 states, so it is not exactly a new idea. They all have different standards, so you cannot get anything going nationally. But it is a consumer protection provision in the law that has already saved consumers billions of dollars. Now, in South Dakota that is not a lot of money, but in West Virginia, that is big time.

Whether you call it the MLR Law or the 80/20 rule that is responsible for hundreds of thousands of rebate checks, including one to my dear sister, that American families and small businesses have been receiving from their health insurance companies for the past 2 years. That is not something that you see every day, an insurance company giving a premium dollar back to its customers.

I understand there are people in this country—probably not in this room, but potentially—who find it hard to concede that anything good has or will come from the Affordable Care Act. But I think it is pretty clear at this point that this piece of law is working, and it is on the way. It is not yet everything we hope for because there have to be more adjustments. That is in the nature of really, really important bills. But it is working, and people are beginning to understand that.

Now, to understand why we have this law, you have to remember that the commercial health insurance market worked before we passed the ACA. It was a market whose rules were rigged against consumers. Insurers could purge sick people from those rolls—I had many examples of that from my own experience in West Virginia—and deny coverage to people with what they call preexisting conditions.

In the old health insurance marketplace, it was very difficult for consumers to compare products or choose plans because the insurers would not give us clear information about coverage and about costs. The Commerce Committee's work back in 2009 played a key role in exposing yet another problem with the health insurance market. Many of the policies health insurance companies were selling to families and businesses, they just were not giving any good value.

We used the industry's own data to make this point. We looked at the percentage of every premium dollar health insurance was spending on healthcare versus the percentage they were spending on administration, commissions, dividends, and other non-healthcare related items. In the health insurance industry, this measurement is called medical ratio.

What we found back in 2009 was a mixed bag. In some markets, insurers were efficiently spending 90 cents or more of each premium dollar on patient care. Let that be understood. Some were doing it right. But in other markets, especially the market for the individual health insurance, the numbers were shockingly low. Some insurance companies were pocketing as much as 50 cents on every premium dollar.

We also found that large national insurers selling the same products across states provided consumers in some states substantially lower value for their premium dollars than in other states. When we talked to industry experts, like Wendell Potter, who is seated before me and Senator John Thune, we learned that the big for-profit insurance companies carefully tracked their MLRs and worked relentlessly to lower them. Their thinking was pretty simple: the less they spend on healthcare, the more they had for their shareholders. It was a zero sum game that pitted patients against profits. And the patients were not winning.

To counter this strong incentive to provide less care to their consumers, we told the health insurance companies that they needed to spend at least 80 cents of each premium dollar on their consumers' healthcare, which would be measured, which would be understood and tracked at HHS, 85 percent in the large group market. If they spent less than 80 percent on patient care, they had to rebate a proportion of the premium payments back to their customers.

This was not a crazy, made-up idea in Washington. Thirty-four states already had minimum medical loss ratio laws on the books. But because the requirements varied from state to state, health insurance companies could still sell low value products in many markets. And we have to do this nationally. We have to make sure that it is fair for everybody.

As always happens when you propose a pro-consumer reform like this, the industry went berserk and predicted dire consequences. Oh, boy, did they do that. A coalition of health insurance companies, agents, and broker groups, and industry friendly insurance commissioners fought this law at every step of the way. And I have to insert here, Senator Klobuchar, that West Virginia at the time had this wonderful person called Jane Cline, who is chairing the National Association of Insurance Commissioners. And she, along with Wendell Potter and others, helped block this effort to undo what we had done.

I will not take time now to detail how much time and money the opponents of the MLR law spent trying to kill it, but my staff has prepared a report on this legislative history of the MLR law, which I now ask unanimous consent to place in the record of this hearing.

[The information referred to follows:]

COMMITTEE ON COMMERCE, SCIENCE, AND TRANSPORTATION

Office of Oversight and Investigations—Majority Staff

DELIVERING CONSUMERS BETTER HEALTH CARE VALUE FOR THEIR PREMIUM DOLLARS: THE SUCCESS STORY OF THE MINIMUM MEDICAL LOSS RATIO LAW

Staff Report for Chairman Rockefeller—May 21, 2014

Table of Contents

4. 2011: Additional NAIC Review Regarding Excluding Agent and Broker Commissions

a. March, 15, 2011, Letter from Chairman Rockefeller to Commissioner Susan E. Voss

b. Spring 2011 NAIC Meeting Austin, Texas

c. May 24, 2011, Committee Majority Staff Report on 2010 MLR Rebates

d. November 21, 2011, Letter from Chairman Rockefeller to Commissioner Kevin McCarty

e. NAIC Endorses Modified McCarty Resolution

III. Conclusion

Exhibits

Exhibit A: Correspondence of Chairman Rockefeller

Exhibit B: Committee Majority Staff Reports

———

Executive Summary

One of the important new consumer protections in the 2010 Affordable Care Act (ACA) is the provision that gives health insurance companies a strong financial incentive to reduce their administrative costs and spend a larger part of each premium dollar on high-quality health care for their policyholders.

Using a financial metric already very familiar to insurance carriers and state regulators—the "medical loss ratio" (MLR)—the law encourages health insurance companies to spend at least 80 percent of their individual and small group policyholders' premiums on medical care or on improving the quality of their care; for large group policies, the target level is 85 percent. The purpose of this law is to counteract health insurance companies' strong financial incentive to maximize profits, even at the expense of their customer's health care. Companies whose spending on health care-related expenses falls below these "minimum MLR" levels are required to pay rebates to their policyholders.

The law also contains important reporting and transparency provisions. For the first time, it requires health insurance companies to publicly report—by market segment and by state—how much of each insurance premium dollar they are spending on health care versus other expenditures such as marketing, agent and broker commissions, overhead, and profits. Hearings and investigations conducted by Chairman Rockefeller in the Commerce Committee in 2009 established a very clear record that health insurance companies were not voluntarily providing American consumers the segment and state-level information they needed to make informed choices about buying health care. These reporting provisions give consumers and policymakers unprecedented amounts of information about the value of the health insurance products sold in their communities.

During the consideration and implementation of the ACA, health insurance companies and groups representing health insurance agents and brokers aggressively opposed the MLR language, which has come to be known as the "80/20 rule." They predicted that the law would harm patients by discouraging investment and innovation, and by reducing health insurance information and the product choices available to consumers. After enactment of the ACA, the health insurance industry also heavily lobbied Congress, the Department of Health and Human Services (HHS), and the National Association of Insurance Commissioners (NAIC) to make adjustments to address these concerns.

During a sometimes contentious implementation process, Chairman Rockefeller and other consumer advocates urged regulators to reject industry proposals that were inconsistent with Congress's intent and reduced the law's potential benefits for consumers. In particular, consumer advocates fought back a last-ditch effort in 2011 to remove agent and broker fees from the denominator of the MLR formula—a seemingly technical change that would have resulted in increased payments to brokers and agents at the expense of dollars being spent on customers' health care and costing consumers hundreds of millions of dollars in lost rebates.

Industry's dire predictions have not materialized, and two years of data shows that the law has worked as the authors of the law intended. Under the new minimum MLR requirements, health insurance companies—especially those selling products in the individual market—have increased the value of their products by offering plans that pay more for health services instead of other expenditures. Since ACA enactment, minimum MLRs have risen across all market segments. The table below represents this aggregated rise in MLRs by market segment, for the six largest for-profit health insurers.

Publicly Traded Health Insurance MLR, 2012 versus 2011

	2011	2012	Change
Individual	77.8%	81.2%	336bp
Small Group	77.2%	77.7%	50bp
Large Group	84.0%	85.2%	115bp

Consumers have benefited from these improvements in several ways:

- *Rebates.* Millions of American consumers and businesses have received $1.6 billion in rebate checks from their health insurance companies because the insurers' coverage fell below the 80 and 85 percent MLR thresholds. This figure does not include 2013 rebates, which will be announced later in 2014.
- *Other Consumer Savings.* Millions more have benefited from the changes health insurers have been making to avoid paying rebates. For example, reports issued by the non-partisan Commonwealth Fund have found that, in the first two years of the MLR requirements, insurers reduced overhead by a total of $1.75 billion—changes that ultimately reduce the cost of insurance to consumers and the government.
- *Reduced State-by-State Subsidization.* Prior to the ACA, health insurers could offer similar health plans in different states but with vastly different MLRs, and companies could make greater profits from plans offered in states that had limited or no MLR requirements. The ACA's new national minimum MLR requirements incentivize health insurers to provide policyholders appropriate value for their premium dollars—no matter what the consumer's state of residence.
- *Increased Transparency.* A new trove of data regarding insurance plan performance is now available to help academics, health policy experts, financial analysts, and others understand how the market is working and where improvements are most necessary.

I. The Value of Medical Loss Ratio Requirements

A. The Role of the MLR

Consumers purchase health insurance for access to emergency and preventative medical services and to protect against the financial risks associated with a traumatic medical event. Health insurers collect premiums from policyholders and use those funds to pay for member health care claims, as well as administer benefit coverage, market health insurance products, and pay dividends to investors. The medical loss ratio (MLR) is the proportion of health care premium dollars paid by consumers that is ultimately spent by insurers on health care costs, versus insurers' other expenses. For example, an insurer with an 80 percent MLR spends 80 percent of its policyholders' premiums on medical care, while the remaining 20 percent goes to expenses that do not directly benefit consumers, such as executive bonuses, advertising costs, agent commissions, and profits.

The MLR is a measure that provides different functions for different constituencies. For consumers, the MLR provides a means of evaluating health plans competing for consumer business. The MLR assists potential purchasers of insurance in assessing whether an insurer is spending an appropriate portion of premiums on consumer medical services. From a consumer's perspective, a higher MLR is an indication of a health insurer spending more premium dollars on services that have greater potential consumer benefits.

For investors in health insurance companies, on the other hand, the MLR provides a measure of an insurer's potential profitability. From an investor's perspective, a decrease in the MLR signals reduction in expenditures on medical costs, and with an adequate control of other indirect medical costs, the possibility for an increase in profit.

For both consumers and investors, segmenting MLR information by insurance market type—individual, small group, and large group—provides additional transparency into the insurance market.[1] As noted by Mark Hall, Professor of Law and Public Health at Wake Forest University, the different insurance markets are "as distinct in their economic and legal characteristics as are mobile homes, condominiums, and single-family homes."[2] MLRs can also vary dramatically based on product type; for instance, in the past MLRs typically have been higher in larger group markets than in the individual market.[3] In contrast, plans marketed as "limited benefit" or "mini-med" typically held lower MLRs than more comprehensive individual health insurance plans.[4]

Health insurers have historically resisted making disclosures of their MLRs or the information relevant to calculating the insurer's MLR. Prior to the Affordable Care Act (ACA), whether an insurer's MLR data was publicly available depended on state regulation. Some states collected and made MLR information available for insurance shoppers, but many did not.[5] In addition, MLR data provided by health insurers to investors was not routinely made available by market segment.[6]

B. The Affordable Care Act's Medical Loss Ratio Requirements

The ACA[7] includes MLR requirements designed to improve the value consumers receive for their health insurance payments and promote transparency in the health insurance market. Under the ACA, individual and small group insurance plans must achieve an 80 percent MLR, while large group plans must achieve 85 percent.[8] The ACA also requires that each insurer publicly disclose its MLR data, including premium income and expenditures on medical claims, broken down by market and state.[9] The provision applies to all types of health insurers that offer fully funded health plans, including non-profit and for-profit health insurers and health management organizations (HMOs).[10] Grandfathered health insurance plans are not excluded from the requirement.[11]

Under the ACA, a health insurer is required to provide its policyholders with rebates if the insurer does not meet the minimum MLR. Rebates are calculated based on an insurer's MLR in a market segment of a given state. Thus, while an insurer could exceed the minimum MLR in a state's large group market, it could still owe

---

[1] American consumers are insured either through their employer, a private health plan, Medicaid, Medicare, the Children's Health Insurance Program (CHIP), the Veteran's Administration, or uninsured. The Henry J. Kaiser Family Foundation, *Health Insurance Coverage of the Total Population* (accessed May 12, 2014) (online at *http://kff.org/other/state-indicator/total-population/*). In 2012, 78.5 million consumers were in fully insured plans regulated by the MLR provision. Carl McDonald and Sahil Choudhry, Citi, *Managed Care: Nothing is More Creative Than a Brilliant Mind with a Purpose,* at 4 (Apr. 8, 2014). A fully insured plan is one where the employer contracts with another organization to assume financial responsibility for the enrollees' medical claims and for all incurred administrative costs. Bureau of Labor Statistics, *Definitions of Health Insurance Terms* (online at *http://www.bls.gov/ncs/ebs/sp/healthterms.pdf*).

[2] Mark A. Hall, *HIPPA's Small-Group Access Laws: Win, Loss, or Draw?,* Cato Journal, at 72 (Spring/Summer 2002).

[3] Senate Committee on Commerce, Science, and Transportation, *Majority Staff Report on Implementing Health Insurance Reform: New Medical Loss Ratio Information for Policymakers and Consumers* (Apr. 15, 2010). Exhibit A includes this report in addition to all other Commerce Committee majority staff reports concerning the MLR, in chronological order, beginning in 2010.

[4] Timothy Jost, *Implementing Health Reform: Fine-Tuning the Medical Loss Ratio Rules,* Health Affairs Blog (Dec. 3, 2011) (online at *http://healthaffairs.org/blog/2011/12/03/implementing-health-reform-fine-tuning-the-medical-loss-ratio-rules/*).

[5] *See* Letter from Chairman John D. Rockefeller to H. Edward Hanway, Chairman and Chief Executive Officer, CIGNA, at 11 (Nov. 2, 2009). Exhibit B includes this letter in addition to all other correspondence by Chairman Rockefeller concerning the MLR, in chronological order, beginning in 2009.

[6] *Id.*

[7] Sec. 2718 of Title XXVII, Part A of the Public Health Service Act, as added by Sec. 10101(a) of Title X of the Patient Protection and Affordable Care Act, Pub. L. 111–148 (2010) (hereafter "PPACA MLR provision").

[8] 45 C.F.R. § 158.210 (2011).

[9] 45 C.F.R. §§ 158.110–120 (2011).

[10] 45 C.F.R. § 158.101 (2011). Self-funded plans (*i.e.,* where the employer or other plan sponsor pays the cost of health benefits from its own assets) are not considered insurers and are therefore not subject to the MLR provision. The MLR standard does not apply even when an insurer administers the self-funded plan on behalf of an employer or other sponsor. The Henry J. Kaiser Family Foundation, *Explaining Health Care Reform: Medical Loss Ratio (MLR)* (Feb. 2012) (online at *http://kff.org/health-reform/fact-sheet/explaining-health-care-reform-medical-loss-ratio-mlr/*).

[11] 45 C.F.R. § 158.102 (2011). Grandfathered plans are those that were in existence on or before March 23, 2010, and whose plan design has stayed basically the same. They can enroll people after that date and still maintain their grandfathered status, meaning that they are not subject to requirements established by the ACA. Kaiser Health News, *FAQ Grandfathered Health Plans* (Nov. 13, 2013) (online at *http://www.kaiserhealthnews.org/stories/2012/december/17/grandfathered-plans-faq.aspx*).

rebates to consumers if it fails to meet the MLR for the individual or small group market in that state. The distribution of rebates depends on the circumstances of the plan. Those consumers who are in the individual market receive rebates directly from the insurer either in the form of a check or as a reduction in future premiums.[12] In the group market, rebates are provided to the employer, who must use the rebate for the benefit of its covered employees.[13]

C. The ACA MLR Provisions Have Benefited Consumers and Small Businesses

The ACA's MLR provisions already have created billions in savings to consumers and small businesses by providing nearly $1.6 billion in rebates and incentivizing insurers to reduce unnecessary health insurer administrative costs and maintain lower premium rates.[14] Further, the reporting requirements of the MLR provisions promote increased insurer transparency and accountability by ensuring that consumers and small businesses have information they can use to measure plan performance and inform insurance shopping decisions. These requirements also provide for a rich source of data that assists experts in analyzing and better understanding the health insurance market.

1. Insurers Have Rebated Hundreds of Millions of Dollars to Consumers and Small Businesses

To date under the ACA, consumers and businesses have received nearly $1.6 billion in rebates from insurers whose MLRs exceeded the ACA thresholds.[15] This includes:

- $591 million in total rebates paid to consumers in the individual market;
- $493 million in total rebates paid to consumers in the small group market; and
- $512 million in total rebates paid to consumers in the large group market.[16]

In 2012, 13.1 million Americans received an average rebate of $137 per family for a total of $1.1 billion in rebates;[17] in 2013, 8.5 million Americans received an average rebate of $100 per family for a total of $500 million in rebates.[18] As discussed below, this decrease between 2012 and 2013 in rebates paid to consumers means that more insurers were meeting the threshold MLRs required by the ACA, and that ultimately more premium dollars were being spent by insurers on health care expenses.

2. Improved Insurer Efficiencies Have Resulted in Additional Savings for Consumers and Small Businesses

Rebates represent only a portion of the savings consumers experience from the MLR. By setting a minimum percentage of expenditures for medical care and quality improvement, the MLR requirements limit what an insurer may expend on overhead, which includes administrative costs and profits. Thus, once the minimum MLR is reached, an insurer has incentive to reduce administrative costs in order to increase profits.[19]

For example, the Commonwealth Fund, a non-partisan research organization, has issued several reports analyzing 2010–2012 insurer data regarding administrative expenditures. According to these analyses, the reduction in insurer overhead—and "ultimately, the cost of insurance to consumers and the government"—was $1.4 billion between 2011 and 2012 and $350 million between 2010 and 2011.[20] These re-

---

[12] 45 C.F.R. § 158.241 (2011).

[13] 45 C.F.R. § 158.242 (2011).

[14] Cynthia Cox, Gary Claxton and Larry Levitt, The Henry J. Kaiser Family Foundation, *Beyond Rebates: How Much are Consumers Saving from the ACA's Medical Loss Ratio Provision?* (June 2013) (online at *http://kff.org/health-reform/perspective/beyond-rebates-how-much-are-consumers-saving-from-the-acas-medical-loss-ratio-provision/*).

[15] United States Department of Health and Human Services, *80/20 Rule Delivers More Value to Consumers in 2012* (June 2013) (hereafter "80/20 Rule Delivers More Value to Consumers").

[16] *Id.*

[17] United States Department of Health and Human Services, *The 80/20 Rule: How Insurers Spend Your Health Insurance Premiums* (Feb. 2013).

[18] 80/20 Rule Delivers More Value to Consumers, *supra* n.15.

[19] Administrative expenses consist of general and administrative expenses, commissions and advertising expenses, profit and contingencies, and various other expenses that do not directly fund medical care. Centers for Medicare and Medicaid Services (CMS), *Medical Loss Ratio (MLR) Annual Reporting Form Filing Instructions for the 2013 MLR Reporting Year* (Mar. 26, 2014).

[20] Michael J. McCue and Mark A. Hall, The Commonwealth Fund, *Realizing Health Reform's Potential—The Federal Medical Loss Ratio Rule: Implications for Consumer in Year 2* (May 14,

Continued

ports cite implementation of the MLR rule as a substantial factor driving insurer overhead reductions.[21]

In June 2013, HHS released an additional study of insurer data from 2011 and 2012 reporting that administrative costs as a percentage of consumer health insurance premiums decreased slightly from 2011 to 2012.[22] The chart below depicts this trend across the various markets.

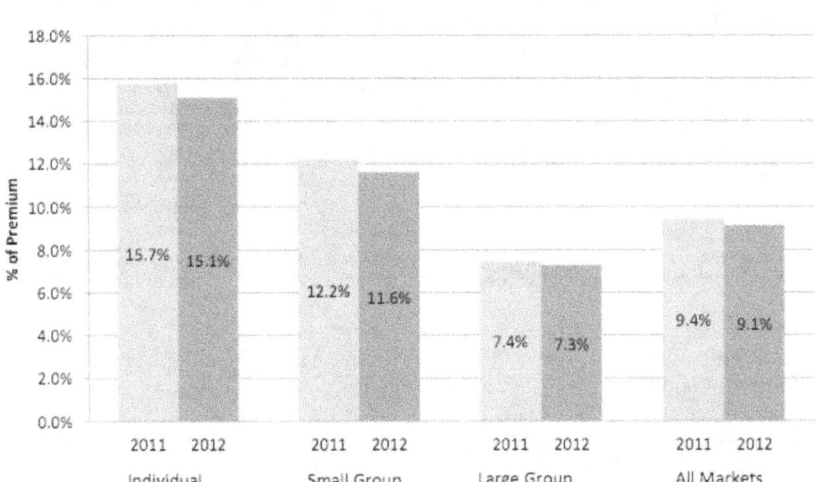

Source: HHS

Experts at The Henry L. Kaiser Family Foundation, a non-partisan health research organization, also have found that, beyond receiving rebates, consumers are receiving better value for their premium dollars as health insurers across all three market segments achieve compliance with the new MLR requirements.[23] And in a separate analysis, HHS estimated what consumer premiums in 2012 would have been if MLRs of health insurers had remained at 2011 levels, finding that Americans saved $3.4 billion on their premiums in 2012 as insurance companies improved efficiencies.[24]

3. Minimum National MLR Standard Means Reduced State-by-State Subsidization

Prior to the establishment of national minimum MLR levels, MLR requirements varied from state to state. Under this patchwork of state laws, health insurers could in effect subsidize their efforts to meet the high MLRs mandated in some states by spending low percentages of consumer premium dollars on medical care in other states that lacked meaningful MLR requirements. For instance, in 2009, WellPoint's small group health insurance product in New Hampshire had an MLR of 87.9 percent but a similar product in Virginia had an MLR of 66.6 percent.[25] By setting a national floor regarding insurer expenditures on medical care, the ACA's MLR re-

2014); Michael J. McCue and Mark A. Hall, The Commonwealth Fund, *Insurers' Responses to Regulation of Medical Loss Ratios*, at 7 (Dec. 2012). The 2012 report also cites other factors in addition to the MLR rule including competitive and state regulatory factors, which may drive insurers' pricing decisions and operational strategies. *Id.* at 3.

[21] Michael J. McCue and Mark A. Hall, The Commonwealth Fund, *Realizing Health Reform's Potential—The Federal Medical Loss Ratio Rule: Implications for Consumer in Year 2* (May 14, 2014); Michael J. McCue and Mark A. Hall, The Commonwealth Fund, *Insurers' Responses to Regulation of Medical Loss Ratios*, at 7 (Dec. 2012).

[22] 80/20 Rule Delivers More Value to Consumers, *supra* n.15.

[23] Cynthia Cox, Gary Claxton and Larry Levitt, The Henry J. Kaiser Family Foundation, *Beyond Rebates: How Much are Consumers Saving from the ACA's Medical Loss Ratio Provision?* (June 2013) (online at *http://kff.org/health-reform/perspective/beyond-rebates-how-much-are-consumers-saving-from-the-acas-medical-loss-ratio-provision/*).

[24] 80/20 Rule Delivers More Value to Consumers, *supra* n.15.

[25] Senate Committee on Commerce, Science, and Transportation, *Majority Staff Report on Implementing Health Insurance Reform: New Medical Loss Ratio Information for Policymakers and Consumers*, at 6 (Apr. 15, 2010).

quirement incentivizes insurers to provide consumers a high value for their premium dollar—regardless of the state in which a consumer may reside.

A recent analysis by Carl McDonald, a leading health insurance industry analyst with Citi, demonstrates the substantial gains consumers have experienced since establishment of the nationwide MLR.[26] Over the course of the last two years, publicly traded health insurers have seen their MLRs rise across the board. The six largest publicly traded health insurers—Aetna, CIGNA, Health Net, Humana, UnitedHealth Group, and WellPoint—operate in state markets across the country. In 2011, these publicly traded health insurance companies met the MLR on an aggregated level in only 4 out of 18 market segments. In 2012, the insurers met the minimum MLR requirements in 10 out of 18 market segments.

Figure 2. Commercial Risk Medical Loss Ratios, 2012 Versus 2011

| | Medical Loss Ratio | | | | | | | | | | | |
| | Individual | | | Small Group | | | Large Group | | | Total | | |
	2011	2012	Change	2011	2012	Change	2011	2012	Change	2011	2012	Change
Aetna Inc.	76.2%	81.9%	567 bp	78.5%	82.0%	346 bp	81.0%	84.6%	358 bp	79.8%	83.6%	374 bp
Cigna Corp.	75.6%	101.8%	2618 bp	85.3%	80.6%	-461 bp	83.7%	84.6%	94 bp	83.4%	85.6%	217 bp
Health Net Inc.	85.4%	90.3%	494 bp	78.6%	81.0%	241 bp	87.0%	91.3%	433 bp	84.8%	88.6%	378 bp
Humana Inc.	72.3%	75.2%	284 bp	74.7%	74.9%	23 bp	82.0%	83.9%	187 bp	77.7%	78.9%	111 bp
UnitedHealth Group Inc.	79.5%	80.8%	133 bp	75.2%	75.8%	57 bp	81.9%	82.1%	16 bp	79.7%	80.0%	27 bp
WellPoint Inc.	78.2%	80.1%	199 bp	78.7%	77.6%	-112 bp	87.3%	87.7%	31 bp	83.9%	84.1%	22 bp
Total Publicly-traded	77.8%	81.2%	336 bp	77.2%	77.7%	50 bp	84.0%	85.2%	115 bp	81.6%	82.7%	116 bp
Total Industry	81.2%	83.6%	249 bp	79.8%	80.8%	104 bp	86.5%	87.3%	85 bp	84.3%	85.4%	107 bp

Source: National Association of Insurance Commissioners and Citi Research

Source: Citi

4. MLR Requirements Have Promoted Transparency

For years before the passage of the ACA, consumers paying a monthly medical insurance premium saw their premiums increase annually but had no window into how their health insurance plans were spending premium dollars. The MLR provisions of the ACA promote transparency in the health insurance marketplace by requiring that insurance companies publicly disclose how they spend consumers' premiums dollars. This national reporting requirement means consumers can access data that was previously unreported or available only to state insurance regulators.

Under the ACA, all health insurers are now required to report to HHS aggregated state-level financial data including income from premiums and expenditures on health care claims, quality improvement, taxes, licensing, and regulatory fees.[27] Health insurers report their MLRs at the state level, across all plans, and in each market segment in which they operate. HHS then makes this data publicly available on its website.[28] This data helps consumers gauge the value they are receiving for their premium dollars. In addition, policy experts, financial market participants, regulators, and other researchers now have access to robust insurer data to assess health insurance market activity.

A case in point is comments of a financial analyst who recently used the new MLR data to evaluate commercial risk issues, noting:

> The data set in this report is quite versatile. . . . [T]he data provides specific details on the states where plans could have too much overlap and run into antitrust issues. And just recently, we were able to analyze the plans that could benefit the most from favorable weather based on where they have the most risk enrollees.[29]

II. A History of the ACA MLR

From the outset of Senator Rockefeller's tenure as Chairman of the Senate Committee on Commerce, Science, and Transportation ("the Committee"), Senator Rockefeller and the Committee have closely scrutinized the health insurance industry's business practices and their impact on consumers. Throughout the health reform debate, the Committee held a series of hearings examining the many obstacles consumers faced when they attempted to make informed purchasing decisions in the

---

[26] Carl McDonald and Sahil Choudhry, Citi, *Managed Care: Nothing is More Creative Than a Brilliant Mind with a Purpose* (Apr. 8, 2014).

[27] 45 C.F.R. § 158.120 (2011).

[28] Centers for Medicare & Medicaid Services, The Center for Consumer Information and Insurance Oversight—Medical Loss Ratio Data and System Resources Home Page (online at *http://www.cms.gov/CCIIO/Resources/Data-Resources/mlr.html*).

[29] Carl McDonald and Sahil Choudhry, Citi, *Managed Care: Nothing is More Creative Than a Brilliant Mind with a Purpose*, at 4 (Apr. 8, 2014).

health insurance market. The hearings demonstrated that one of the greatest difficulties consumers faced was getting clear and accurate information about health insurance products. The Committee also examined several abusive health insurance practices that focused on how insurers would often take advantage of policyholders while in the pursuit of higher profits.[30]

In 2009, during the development of health insurance reform legislation, the Committee's investigations and oversight work regarding the health insurance industry provided impetus for the MLR requirements that ultimately were included in the ACA. Following enactment of the ACA, Chairman Rockefeller continued vigilant oversight of MLR implementation to make sure consumers and small businesses receive appropriate value for their premiums, and have the information they need to make informed decisions about health plans for themselves and their families. Following is a chronicle of these efforts.

A. The Health Reform Debate and the MLR

1. June 2009: Commerce Committee Hearing

On June 24, 2009, the Commerce Committee held a hearing titled "Consumer Choices and Transparency in the Health Insurance Industry" to examine obstacles American consumers face when attempting to obtain clear and accurate information about their health insurance coverage. At that hearing, one of the witnesses, former CIGNA executive Wendell Potter, argued that health insurers had strong incentives to minimize the amount spent on actual medical care in order to promote greater company profits.

Drawing on experiences from his over 20-year career as a senior health insurance industry executive, Mr. Potter testified about the pressure health insurance companies felt from Wall Street to keep medical loss ratios low:

> I have seen an insurer's stock price fall 20 percent or more in a single day after executives disclosed that the company had to spend a slightly higher percentage of premiums on medical claims during the quarter than it did during a previous period. The smoking gun was the company's first-quarter medical loss ratio, which had increased from 77.9 percent to 79.4 percent a year later.[31]

Mr. Potter also asserted that health insurers used techniques to trim their MLRs including dumping and purging sick policyholders to reduce the number of expensive policy holders needing expensive care.[32] Further, Mr. Potter highlighted a 2008 PricewaterhouseCoopers study showing how successful the health insurance industry had become in charging more for health insurance while paying a decreasing share on actual medical care:

> The accounting firm found that the collective medical-loss ratios of the seven largest for-profit insurers fell from an average of 85.3 percent in 1998 to 81.6 percent in 2008. That translates into a difference of several billion dollars in favor of insurance company shareholders and executives at the expense of health care providers and their patients.[33]

2. August 2009: Chairman Rockefeller's Letters to Insurance Company Executives

Following the June 2009 Committee hearing, Chairman Rockefeller wrote to 15 of the largest health insurance companies to further examine MLRs in the individual, small, and large group markets, and how the health insurance industry collects, uses, and publicizes MLR information. These companies collectively controlled

---

[30] As Chairman of the Senate Committee on Commerce, Science, and Transportation, Senator Rockefeller has examined the consumer perspective in the American health insurance market. *See* Senate Committee on Commerce, Science, and Transportation, *Hearings on Part I: Deceptive Health Insurance Industry Practices—Are Consumers Getting What They Paid For?* (Mar. 26, 2009); Senate Committee on Commerce, Science, and Transportation, *Hearings on Part II: Deceptive Health Insurance Industry Practices—Are Consumers Getting What They Paid For?* (Mar. 31, 2009); Senate Committee on Commerce, Science, and Transportation, *Hearings on Competition in the Health Care Marketplace* (July 16, 2009); Senate Committee on Commerce, Science, and Transportation, *Hearings on Are Mini Med Policies Really Health Insurance?* (Dec. 1, 2010); Senate Committee on Commerce, Science, and Transportation, *Staff Report on Underpayments to Consumers by the Health Insurance Industry* (June 24, 2009)

[31] Senate Committee on Commerce, Science, and Transportation, Testimony of Wendell Potter, *Consumer Choices and Transparency in the Health Insurance Industry,* 111th Cong. (June 24, 2009) (S. Rept. 111–344) at 8.

[32] *Id.*

[33] *Id.* at 9.

more than half of the Nation's fully insured marketplace.[34] The letters sought information on how the companies spent their policyholders' premium dollars, noting that while the MLR is a key tool for understanding the health insurance market, "insurance companies do not appear to readily disclose this information to consumers and businesses."[35]

3. September–October 2009: Senate Committee on Finance Markup of Health Reform Legislation

As the Committee was seeking MLR information from health insurers, from late September through early October 2009, the Senate Finance Committee, on which Senator Rockefeller serves as the Chair of the Subcommittee on Health, began consideration of health reform law legislation.[36] At the time of this legislative markup, Chairman Rockefeller had received incomplete responses to his August letters to health insurers requesting MLR information.

Noting recalcitrance among insurers in providing transparency on consumer premium expenditures, Chairman Rockefeller proposed an amendment establishing an 85 percent MLR for insurers that participate in the health markets—or "exchanges"—established under the Act.[37] This amendment was based on freestanding legislation introduced in the Senate Committee on Health, Education, Labor, and Pensions the same week by Senator Franken, and cosponsored by Sens. Rockefeller, Whitehouse, Sanders, Begich, Stabenow, and Leahy.[38] During the Senate Finance Committee markup, Senator Rockefeller explained the rationale for establishing minimum national MLR requirements:

> That would seem to me to be a reasonable and fair requirement for a health insurance company whose business in public life is to provide health insurance with premiums that go back and forth. But regardless of what those premiums might be, the majority of the premiums, the majority of what they make is spent on medical care for the people that they are in business to insure.[39]

Ultimately, the amendment was pulled from consideration since the Congressional Budget Office (CBO) had not yet provided an evaluation of its cost.[40]

4. November 2009: Letter from Chairman Rockefeller to CIGNA

While many health insurers that were either not-for-profit or that operated primarily in just one state provided Chairman Rockefeller complete responses to his August 2009 request for MLR data, many for-profit health insurers did not. Seeking further understanding of expenditures within this market, the Commerce Committee obtained MLR filing data for 2008 and 2009 submitted by the 15 largest for-profit health insurers to the National Association of Insurance Commissioners

---

[34] A fully insured plan is one where the employer contracts with another organization to assume financial responsibility for the enrollees' medical claims and for all incurred administrative costs. Bureau of Labor Statistics, *Definitions of Health Insurance Terms* (online at http://www.bls.gov/ncs/ebs/sp/healthterms.pdf).

[35] Letter from Chairman John D. Rockefeller to Stephen J. Hemsley, President and Chief Executive Officer, UnitedHealth Group, at 1 (Aug. 21, 2009).

[36] Shailagh Murray and Lori Montgomery, *Lines Drawn as Senate Panel Begins Debating Health Bill,* Washington Post (Sept. 23, 2009) (online at *http://www.washingtonpost.com/wp-dyn/content/article/2009/09/22/AR2009092201548.html*). This measure, the "America's Healthy Future Act," ultimately introduced as S. 1796, was one of two major bills being considered by the Senate as part of health reform. The second, the "Affordable Health Choices Act," S.1679, was reported out of the Committee on Health, Education, Labor, and Pensions on September 17, 2009.

[37] Senate Committee on Finance, *Results of Executive Session, America's Health Future Act of 2009* (Sept. 22, 2009) (online at *http://www.finance.senate.gov/legislation/details/?id=61f4fb98-a3d0-d85c-d33f-f2c598e1d138*).

[38] S. 1730, 111th Cong. (2009).

[39] Senate Committee on Finance, *Continuation of the Open Executive Sessions to Consider an Original Bill Providing for Health Care Reform,* at 195, 111th Cong. (Oct. 1, 2009).

[40] *Id.* at 219.Ce ine at (nk doesn'tee on Health, Education, Labor, and Pensions ffordable Care Acte comprehensive plans.."

(NAIC)[41] pursuant to various state requirements.[42] Committee majority staff examined this data in conjunction with data publicly filed with the Securities and Exchange Commission (SEC) over the same time period.

This review found a discrepancy between the MLR information the insurance industry provided to consumers and policy makers versus the MLR information provided to investors during the health reform debate. Specifically, in December 2008, America's Health Insurance Plans (AHIP) issued a report showing an industry-wide MLR of 87 percent in 2008.[43] Based on the findings of this report, AHIP created the below figure showing that 87 cents out of every 100 is spent on medical care leaving 13 cents for non-medical expenses and profit.

However, SEC filings of the six largest publicly-traded health insurers (including CIGNA) showed that none of the health insurers achieved the 87 percent MLR that the AHIP report cited. In these SEC filings, which are public documents but are targeted to investors and potential investors who are interested in a company's profitability, the companies' reported 2008 MLRs ranged from 81.5 percent to a high of 84.8 percent.[44]

When multiplied across the $70 billion health insurers collected in premiums in 2008 alone, these discrepancies in MLR percentages amounted to billions of dollars.[45] Chairman Rockefeller discussed concerns raised by this analysis in a November 2, 2009, letter to the chief executive officer of CIGNA,[46] and CIGNA subsequently refiled its policy exhibits with the NAIC to correct the inaccurate information identified by Chairman Rockefeller.

5. December 2009: Senate Passage of Health Reform Legislation with MLR Provisions

In November 2009, the full Senate took up debate of health reform legislation. Senator Rockefeller successfully pressed for inclusion in the leadership amendment package MLR language similar to what he had proposed in the Senate Finance Committee health reform markup and to what Senator Franken had introduced in his stand-alone bill. The amendment established a minimum MLR of 80 percent for

---

[41] NAIC is the U.S. standard-setting and regulatory support organization created and governed by the chief insurance regulators from the 50 states, the District of Columbia and five U.S. territories. Through the NAIC, state insurance regulators establish standards and best practices, conduct peer review, and coordinate their regulatory oversight. National Association of Insurance Commissioners, *About the NAIC* (online at http://www.naic.org/index_about.htm).

[42] State Insurance Commissioners require health insurers to file detailed financial disclosures with the NAIC for solvency purposes. As part of these filings, information pertaining to a plan's pre ACA MLR was available.

[43] PricewaterhouseCoopers, *The Factors Fueling Rising Health Care Costs 2008,* Prepared for AHIP, at 2 (Dec. 2008).

[44] Letter from Chairman John D. Rockefeller to H. Edward Hanway, Chairman and Chief Executive Officer, CIGNA, at 7 (Nov. 2, 2009).

[45] *Id.*

[46] *Id.* at 15.

the individual and small group health insurance segments, and 85 percent for the large group segment.

The decision to establish minimum medical loss ratios at these levels was guided by the CBO's determination that the majority of insurers were already providing benefits to their customers at or above these levels.[47]

During Senate floor consideration of the leadership amendment package, Senator Bill Nelson from Florida spoke to the legislative intent of the proposed MLR language. Sharing his experiences as a past state insurance commissioner of Florida, Senator Nelson stated:

> For 6 years, I got to see what insurance companies will do. I can tell you. Instead of 85 percent and 80 percent that we are going to require in this bill of every insurance premium dollar they pay out in medical care. I can tell you that some of the insurance companies I regulated back in the State of Florida were down in the sixties. A lot of that was going into big-time administrative offices, all kinds of jets, all kinds of padded expense accounts. . . .

> We need to ensure that the policyholder's premiums and the Federal subsidies that are going into the purchase of private health insurance on the exchange are used for actual medical care and not for wasteful administrative spending and marketing and profits. If we don't do this kind of thing, regulating insurance companies, they are going to take advantage. They are going to take advantage of making more money at the expense of patient care.[48]

The Senate passed the MLR amendment on December 22, 2009,[49] and passed the bill containing this amendment on December 24, 2009.[50] The MLR provisions remained in the final version enacted by Congress after the Senate and House resolved differences between their versions of the bill.[51]

B. Implementation of the Affordable Care Act MLR Provisions

1. Elements of the MLR Formula

Prior to passage of the ACA, the MLR was a calculation that served mainly to provide the shareholders of for-profit health insurance companies with some indication of how much profit the insurer was making. Under the pre-ACA—or "traditional"—MLR definition, the numerator consisted of the company's expenditures for health care claims and the denominator consisted of the company's total premium intake. The ACA MLR definition differs from the traditional MLR calculation in several ways: (1) it allows a category of expenses considered to involve "quality improvement" to be counted in the numerator; and (2) it allows for a reduction in the denominator reflecting taxes and fees.[52] The figure below demonstrates the difference between a "traditional" MLR and the ACA's MLR.

---

[47] Congressional Budget Office, *Budgetary Treatment of Proposals to Regulate Medical Loss Ratios* (Dec. 13, 2009).

[48] Statement of Senator Bill Nelson, Congressional Record, S13626–13628 (Dec. 20, 2009).

[49] The leadership amendment, S. Amdt. 3276, was introduced on December 19, 2009. *See* Congressional Record, S13491–92. The amendment passed 60–39 on December 22, 2009. *See* Congressional Record, S13716.

[50] U.S. Senate, Roll Call Vote on H.R. 3590 (Dec. 24, 2009) (60 yeas, 39 nays).

[51] The House of Representatives agreed to Senate amendments to the health reform bill on March 21, 2010 by a vote of 219–212. U.S. House of Representatives, Roll Call Vote on H.R. 4872 (Mar. 21, 2010) (219 yeas, 212 nays).

[52] Under the ACA, Federal and state taxes are subtracted from the total amount of premium revenue in the denominator of the MLR ratio. The contours of what constitutes "federal and state taxes," however, were left to the rulemaking process. In the NAIC process, Federal taxes were defined as "all Federal taxes and assessments allocated to health insurance coverage reported under section 2718 of the PHS Act, excluding Federal income taxes on investment income and capital gains." HHS adopted this definition in the interim and final rules, noting that investment income and capital gains taxes "are not taxes based on premium revenues, and thus should not be used to adjust premium revenues." Department of Health and Human Services, *Health Insurance Issuers Implementing Medical Loss Ratio (MLR) Requirements Under the Patient Protection and Affordable Care Act*, 75 Fed. Reg. 74878 (Dec. 1, 2010) (interim final rule).

Traditional and ACA-MLR Formula Comparison

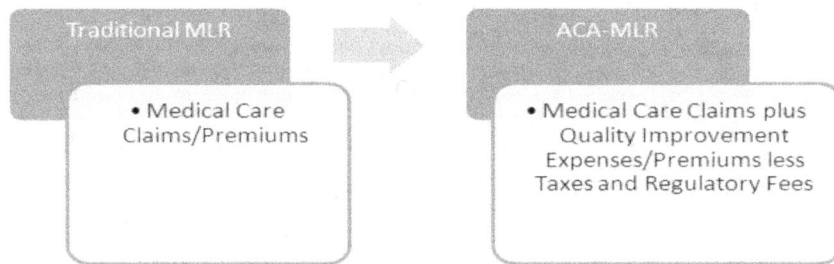

Source: Mark Farrah Associates

The ACA provided that NAIC would develop the new definitions and methodologies that health insurance companies and regulators would use for purposes of determining compliance with the ACA's minimum MLR requirements.[53] The Secretary of the Department of Health and Human Services (HHS) was then tasked with certifying, by December 31, 2010, the MLR definitions and methodologies developed by the NAIC.[54]

2. NAIC Implementation Process

The NAIC set up two working groups of state insurance commissioners to develop the definitions and methodologies required under the ACA's MLR provisions. One group focused on devising a form for insurers to use to report the components of the MLR; the other was responsible for developing the definitions to be used in the MLR reports.[55] Key terms that required definition in this process included "quality improvement activities," the category of costs the ACA's MLR formula allows to be included as part of an insurer's medical costs.[56] As part of its implementation process, the NAIC allowed for participation by interested stakeholders, including insurance company representatives and consumer advocates, providing opportunities to join conference calls and offer written comments.

As the NAIC began the process of determining MLR definitions, consumer advocates and others became concerned that health insurers would work to dilute the MLR in two ways: (1) health insurers might attempt to reclassify certain administrative expenses as medical expenses or use an overly broad definition of "quality improvement expense" that could mask expenses that were actually administrative in nature; and (2) that national aggregation—as opposed to state-level aggregation—of MLR data would allow companies to avoid having to pay rebates to health insurance consumers in states with low MLRs as long as they maintain their MLR above the national level.

Chairman Rockefeller monitored the NAIC implementation process and when appropriate, engaged with the NAIC to push back against efforts by the insurance industry that would have diluted intended consumer benefits of the MLR.

a. April 15, 2010 Committee Majority Staff Report

On April 15, 2010, Chairman Rockefeller released a Commerce Committee majority staff report titled "Implementing Health Insurance Reform: New Medical Loss Ratio Information for Policymakers and Consumers" ("April 2010 report") to provide background on pre-ACA insurer MLRs. The report analyzed the insurance industry's regulatory filings with the NAIC in 2008 and 2009 as well as insurer responses to the Chairman's August 2009 letter inquiries, and examined the importance of segmenting the MLRs by individual, small and large group segments. The report also highlighted the importance of establishing clear limits on the definition of what con-

---

[53] PPACA MLR provision, *supra* n. 7, at 2718(c).

[54] *Id.*

[55] Timothy Jost, *Implementing Health Reform: Medical Loss Ratios,* Health Affairs Blog (Nov. 23, 2010) (online at *http://healthaffairs.org/blog/2010/11/23/implementing-health-reform-medical-loss-ratios/*).

[56] Department of Health and Human Services, *Health Insurance Issuers Implementing Medical Loss Ratio (MLR) Requirements Under the Patient Protection and Affordable Care Act,* 75 Fed. Reg. 74875 (Dec. 1, 2010) (interim final rule).

stitutes a "quality improvement" cost to prevent insurers from manipulating the new MLR formula to the detriment of consumers.[57]

The April 2010 report's analysis of 2008 and 2009 regulatory filings with the NAIC showed that although many health insurers across the country were already meeting the minimum MLRs set forth in the ACA, the largest for-profit health insurers spent a much smaller portion of premium dollars on medical care in the individual market as compared to the larger group markets.[58] According to this analysis, the largest for-profit insurers used about 15 cents out of every large group premium dollar for non-medical expenses while using more than 26 cents out of every premium dollar for non-medical expenses in the individual market.[59] Leading insurer WellPoint provided a case in point. While WellPoint told its investors in 2009 that its overall MLR was 82.6 percent, its individual and small group market insurance products had MLRs of 74.9 percent and 81.2 percent.[60] The table below demonstrates the discrepancies between individual and group plan MLRs discussed in the report.

	Individual		Small Group		Large Group	
	2009	2008	2009	2008	2009	2008
Aetna	75.7%	73.9%	84.2%	82.0%	87.2%	82.0%
CIGNA	88.1%	86.9%	92.1%	—	85.2%	37.2%
Coventry	71.9%	65.8%	78.2%	79.1%	86.0%	82.7%
Humana	68.1%	71.9%	80.0%	77.2%	88.2%	82.4%
UnitedHealth	70.5%	70.3%	81.1%	78.7%	83.3%	83.5%
WellPoint	74.9%	73.1%	81.2%	79.0%	84.9%	85.2%
TOTAL	73.6%	72.5%	81.2%	79.7%	85.1%	83.9%

The April 2010 report also examined data of six large, state-based subsidiaries of WellPoint to assess the expected impact of new MLR requirements at the state level. As shown in the following chart, this data showed substantial variation between states:

	Individual Segment	Small Group Segment	Large Group Segment
Anthem Health Plans of NH	62.9%	87.9%	88.4%
Anthem Health Plans of VA	72.1%	66.6%	79.4%
Rocky Mountain Hospital & Medical	74.1%	79.9%	83.1%
Blue Cross Blue Shield of GA	75.5%	78.0%	86.0%
Anthem Health Plans of KY	79.4%	80.9%	82.0%
Anthem Health Plans of ME	95.2%	86.9%	89.5%

The April 2010 report further raised concerns about how insurers would approach accounting under the new MLR requirements. A separate report issued in the same time frame by health care industry analyst Carl McDonald of Oppenheimer & Co. had highlighted the financial incentive for health insurance companies to shift expenditures from the category of administrative costs to the category of medical costs,[61] suggesting that companies would seek to "MLR shift" their costs from administrative to medical by 5 percent, or 500 basis points.[62] Pointing to this analysis, the Committee majority staff's April 2010 report asserted that a stricter definition of "quality improvement expenses" would limit the ability of health insurers to

---

[57] Senate Committee on Commerce, Science, and Transportation, *Majority Staff Report on Implementing Health Insurance Reform: New Medical Loss Ratio Information for Policymakers and Consumers,* at 5 (Apr. 15, 2010).

[58] *Id.* at 3.

[59] *Id.* at 3–4.

[60] *Id.* at 3.

[61] *See Id.* at 6 citing to Carl McDonald and James Naklicki, Oppenheimer & Co. Inc. Equity Research Industry Update, *The Average Person Thinks He Isn't—Minimum Medical Loss Ratio Analysis* (Apr. 8, 2010).

[62] *Id.*

"MLR shift" and strongly recommended that regulators "remain vigilant and focused on ensuring that consumers get the benefit of the new federally mandated medical loss ratios."[63]

b. May 7, 2010, Letters from Chairman Rockefeller to Secretary Sebelius and NAIC Commissioner Cline

As the NAIC continued its deliberations, Chairman Rockefeller wrote to HHS Secretary Kathleen Sebelius and NAIC Commissioner Jane Cline, then the President of the NAIC, to express his deep concern that the health insurance industry was "mounting an all-out effort" to weaken the MLR. In this letter he reminded policymakers that the intent of the MLR was to make sure that "most of consumers' health insurance premiums dollars should be going to pay for patient care, not for insurers' administrative costs and profits."[64]

Specifically, the Chairman highlighted the importance of requiring MLR reports on a state-by-state and market-by-market basis, as opposed to allowing insurers to report aggregate nationwide MLRs, to make sure consumers in a given state have appropriate information to evaluate their insurance options.[65]

These letters also reiterated the concern that insurers have strong financial incentives to "MLR shift" administrative expenses to the medical side, and argued that cost containment data reported to NAIC in 2009 should be viewed as a reference point in assessing insurer predictions about their quality improvement expenditures. Committee staff analysis of this cost containment data showed that insurers invested an average of just 1.15 percent of their premium dollars on cost containment activities. While noting that cost containment expenses did not precisely overlap with activities that improve health quality, the Chairman argued that the low cost containment expenditures provide grounds for reviewing "with skepticism" proposals that would "allow insurers to claim that they will spend significantly higher portions of premium dollars on quality improvement in the year 2011 than they are currently spending on cost containment."[66]

c. July 20, 2010, Letter from Chairman Rockefeller to Commissioner Cline

On July 20, 2010, Chairman Rockefeller wrote NAIC Commissioner Jane Cline to express concern about mounting evidence of vast imbalances in resources of health insurers versus consumer advocates as they made their case in the NAIC process.[67] In this letter, he also addressed key issues yet to be decided by the NAIC, including the final definition of "quality improvement expenses."[68] At this time, major insurers were arguing against the use of evidence-based standards in defining this term.

In a June 2010 letter, Blue Cross Blue Shield Association (BCBSA) complained to the NAIC that requiring evidence-based standards in the definitions of "quality improvement expenses" would present "unnecessary barriers and unreasonable high standards" for insurers.[69] UnitedHealthcare Group made a similar point in a letter to the NAIC in a letter providing edits to a draft set of definitions, displayed below, that the NAIC had circulated for comment.[70]

---

[63] *Id.* at 7.

[64] Letter from Chairman John D. Rockefeller to Kathleen Sebelius, Secretary, Department of Health and Human Services (May 7, 2010); Letter from Chairman John D. Rockefeller to Commissioner Jane Cline, President, National Association of Insurance Commissioners (May 7, 2010).

[65] *Id.* at 3–4. The letters cited data discussed in the April 2010 report showing variation between market segments and within market segments.

[66] *Id.* at 7.

[67] Letter from Chairman John D. Rockefeller to Commissioner Jane Cline, President, National Association of Insurance Commissioners, at 2 (July 20, 2010).

[68] *Id.* at 3–6.

[69] *Id.* at 5.

[70] *Id.*

Figure 1 - UnitedHealthcare's June 28, 2010, Suggested Edit to the Definition of Quality Improvement Expenses

Improving Health Care Quality Expenses – General Definition:

Quality Improvement (QI) Expenses are expenses, other than those billed or allocated by a provider for care delivery (i.e., clinical or claims costs), for health services that are designed to improve health care quality and increase the likelihood of desired health outcomes in ways that are capable of being objectively measured and which produce verifiable results and achievements.

In his letter to Commissioner Cline, Chairman Rockefeller argued that an evidence-based approach best reflected the law's intent to "improve the safety, timeliness and effectiveness of the care patients receive,"[71] and that without such an approach, health insurance companies could claim any expense they labeled as improving patient quality as a "quality improvement expense." The Chairman cited the following examples of expenditures that insurers were claiming constituted "quality improvements" but that appeared to have questionable impact on improving the quality of care a policyholder could expect to experience:[72]

- The money health insurance companies spend processing and paying claims;
- The money health insurance companies spend creating and maintaining their provider networks;
- The money health insurers spend updating their information technology systems to code medical conditions and process claims payments;
- The money health insurance companies spend to protect against fraud and other threats to the integrity of their payment systems; and
- The money health insurance companies use to conduct "utilization review" of paid claims to detect payments the companies deem inappropriate and retroactively deny them.[73]

The NAIC working group tasked with devising the definition of "quality improving expenses" ultimately insisted that "quality improvement expenses" should be evidenced based, should "advance the delivery of patient-centered care," and should be "capable of being objectively measured."[74]

d. October 14, 2010, Letter from Chairman Rockefeller to the NAIC

In early October 2010, as the NAIC neared the end of its deliberations on the MLR definitions and methodologies, the health insurance industry sought to re-open the debate regarding state versus national level aggregation for health insurance company MLRs. Chairman Rockefeller addressed this argument in an October 14, 2010 letter to Commissioner Cline, urging the NAIC to maintain its "pro-consumer perspective and to reject the health insurance industry's last-minute attempt to erode the good work of the [NAIC]."[75] This lobbying effort by the health insurance industry ultimately failed and the NAIC moved to have its final recommendations sent to the Secretary of HHS.

These NAIC recommendations largely reflected Chairman Rockefeller's input on key issues of requiring a thorough and thoughtful definition of "quality improvement expenses," and the requirement that health insurance plans report their MLR performance at the state level.

3. HHS Rulemaking Process

On October 27, 2010, the NAIC provided its final recommendations to the Secretary of HHS, as directed by Public Health Service Act Section 2718(c).[76] HHS began its implementation process by publishing an interim final rule (IFR) in the

---

[71] *Id.* at 3.

[72] *Id.* at 4.

[73] *Id.*

[74] The NAIC's definition of "quality improving expenses" was ultimately adopted by HHS. *See* Centers for Medicare and Medicaid Services (CMS), *Medical Loss Ratio (MLR) Annual Reporting Form Filing Instructions for the 2013 MLR Reporting Year,* at 14–15, 31 (Mar. 26, 2014).

[75] Letter from Chairman John D. Rockefeller to Commissioner Jane Cline, President, National Association of Insurance Commissioners, at 2 (Oct. 14, 2010).

[76] Letter from the National Association of Insurance Commissioners to Kathleen Sebelius, Secretary, Department of Health and Human Services (Oct. 27, 2010).

Federal Register on December 1, 2010, with request for public comment. The IFR adopted the NAIC recommendations in full,[77] and ultimately, HHS adopted a final rule on December 7, 2011.[78]

While many stakeholder disagreements were resolved in the NAIC process, stakeholders continued to vigorously debate a number of key issues during the HHS rulemaking process, including the issue of how to properly classify "quality improvement expenses." The rulemaking also explored how expenses associated with health insurance agent and broker commission fees were to be accounted.

a. Activities That Improve Health Care Quality

Insurers and other interest groups argued that a broad definition of "quality improvement expenses" would allow for future innovations. Consumer advocates and provider groups, on the other hand, wanted HHS to more concretely define such expenses to prevent health insurers from essentially nullifying the purpose of the minimum MLR by allowing administrative expenses to be deemed "quality improvements."[79]

The final rule ultimately adopted the approach taken by the NAIC, which provides that a quality improvement activity is one designed to improve health quality and increase the likelihood of desired health outcomes in ways that can be objectively measured, is directed toward individual enrollees or incurred for the benefit of specified segments of enrollees, and is grounded in evidence-based medicine or some other widely accepted criteria.[80] The rule also specifies insurer activities that do *not* qualify as quality improvement expenses. These include activities primarily designed to control costs, fraud prevention activities, customer service hotlines addressing non-clinical member questions, and maintenance of a claims adjudication system, among others.[81]

b. Agent and Broker Fees

The IFR included a section of expenses it called "other non-claims costs" to be calculated as non-medical administrative costs. HHS defined these costs as "expenditures that are not used to adjust premiums, incurred claims, or activities that improve quality care."[82] The NAIC included agent and broker fees in this section, and HHS adopted that approach in the IFR. However, because the NAIC had raised concern over the potential impact on the industry from excluding agent and broker fees from the calculation of medical costs, HHS sought comment on this issue.

In elements of the fully insured health insurance market, insurance agents and brokers serve as the marketing and sales conduit through which an individual or small business would purchase a health insurance product. Agents and brokers who sell health insurance typically had been paid on a commission model, meaning as compensation for their services, they received a percentage of the health insurance policyholder's premiums dollars. Insurance agents and brokers believed that keeping their commissions in the MLR calculation of "other non-claims costs" would lead to reduced commissions, as health insurance plans sought to reduce administrative expenses in order to meet the ACA's MLR requirements.[83]

During the comment period, stakeholders addressed the issue of how to classify agent and broker fees. The Council of Insurance Agents & Brokers wrote that agents and brokers provide critical services in the group health insurance market, such as administering benefit programs, assisting with Federal and state legal compliance, and advising on mitigating rising costs.[84] The National Association of Health Underwriters said that the fees should not be considered administrative costs, as they are passed-through fees rather than insurer revenue.[85] The U.S. Chamber of Commerce argued that "agents and brokers serve a critical role in the

---

[77] Department of Health and Human Services, *Medical Loss Ratio Requirement Under the Patient Protection and Affordable Care Act,* 76 Fed. Reg. 76590 (Dec. 7, 2011) (final rule).

[78] *Id.* at 76574.

[79] Department of Health and Human Services, *Medical Loss Ratio Requirement Under the Patient Protection and Affordable Care Act,* 75 Fed. Reg. 74876 (Dec. 1, 2010) (interim final rule).

[80] *Id.* at 74875.

[81] *Id.* at 74875–76.

[82] *Id.* at 74877.

[83] Letter from Ken A. Crerar, President, Council of Insurance Agents & Brokers, President, to the Office of Consumer Information and Insurance Oversight (Jan. 31, 2011).

[84] *Id.* at 2–3.

[85] Letter from Janet Trautwein, Executive Vice President and Chief Executive Officer, National Association of Health Underwriters, to Kathleen Sebelius, Secretary, Department of Health and Human Services, at 2 (Jan. 28, 2011).

health care marketplace by aiding consumers and employers in determining the health plan that best suits their needs at a premium they can afford."[86]

Other stakeholders expressed support for maintaining agent and broker fees as non-claims costs. AARP called for caution with respect to changes in the treatment of such fees as they relate to the MLR. It urged that changes should "be based on objective evidence with the burden of proof on the issuers to justify such fees as anything other than a non-claims cost."[87] The American Medical Association also supported treating broker fees and commissions as non-claims costs, arguing that these are "quintessential administrative costs" that "do not constitute the provision of medical services or the provision of services to improve the quality of those medical services."[88]

Finally, consumer groups expressed concern that "some insurers have already stated that they intend to collect commissions from enrollees on behalf of brokers and agents but to not count the amounts collected as premium revenue or administrative expenses."[89] These groups therefore urged HHS to support the IFR approach to agent and broker costs and to vigilantly enforce the IFR provisions.

The final rule made no changes to the treatment of agent and broker fees. As such, they were defined as costs to be included in the non-claims cost portion of the MLR.

4. 2011: Additional NAIC Review Regarding Excluding Agent and Broker Commissions

The 2010 mid-term elections brought substantial changes to the composition of Congress and state governments, bringing in a number of new members of Congress and state governors who opposed the ACA. The composition of the NAIC also saw substantial change, including the election of four new commissioners.[90] In addition, at this time Florida Insurance Commissioner Kevin McCarty was designated NAIC President-elect, for a term beginning in 2012.[91] Throughout the course of 2011, the NAIC saw renewed efforts by the health insurance industry and its allies at the state and Federal level to roll back key provisions of the ACA including the MLR.

One of the issues that received attention during this period was the earlier NAIC and HHS decision to exclude agent and broker fees from the determination of medical expenses under the MLR formula. Throughout 2011, Chairman Rockefeller monitored the NAIC's reconsideration of whether agent and broker commissions should be exempted from the MLR calculation, and engaged where appropriate with the NAIC on this issue.

a. March 15, 2011, Letter from Chairman Rockefeller to Commissioner Susan E. Voss

As the debate regarding the treatment of health insurance agent and broker commissions gathered momentum, the NAIC's Professional Health Insurance Advisors Task Force took up the issue.[92] This task force was charged with monitoring the impact of the ACA on health insurance agents and brokers, as well as the health insurance consumers and the insurance market they serve.[93] Commissioner McCarty led the task force and on March 3, 2011, in advance of NAIC's planned spring meeting in Austin, Texas, he released draft Federal legislation for public comment. The McCarty Proposal would have excluded agent and broker commissions from the MLR calculation.[94]

---

[86] Letter from Randel K. Johnson, Senior Vice President of Labor, Immigration, & Employee Benefits, and Katie Mahoney, Director of Health Care Regulations, U.S. Chamber of Commerce, to the Office of Consumer Information and Insurance Oversight, at 7 (Jan. 31, 2011).

[87] Letter from David Certner, Legislative Counsel and Legislative Policy Director, AARP, to the Center for Consumer Information and Insurance Oversight, at 3 (Jan. 31, 2011).

[88] Letter from Dr. Michael D. Maves, Executive Vice President and Chief Executive Officer, American Medical Association, to Kathleen Sebelius, Secretary, Department of Health and Human Services, at 2 (Jan. 31, 2011).

[89] Letter from Health Care for America Now to the Office of Consumer Information and Insurance Oversight, at 3.

[90] Chad Hemenway, *Hello. My Name Is. . .,* National Underwriter Property & Casualty (Dec. 20, 2010) (online at *http://www.propertycasualty360.com/2010/12/20/9-hello-my-name-is*).

[91] Sean P. Carr, *NAIC Picks New Leaders in Wake of Electoral Defeat,* A.M. Best Newswire (Dec. 15, 2010) (online at *http://insurancenewsnet.com/oarticle/2010/12/15/naic-picks-new-leaders-in-wake-of-electoral-defeat-a-240090.html#.U3UZvcfBre8*).

[92] National Association of Insurance Commissioners, *Professional Health Insurance Advisors (D) Task Force,* (accessed May 6, 2014) (online at *http://www.naic.org/committees_ d_health_advisors_tf.htm*).

[93] *Id.*

[94] H.R. 1206, 112th Cong. (2012).

Chairman Rockefeller on March 15, 2011, wrote to Commissioner Susan E. Voss, then the President of the NAIC, regarding these renewed attempts to dilute the MLR.[95] This letter highlighted how the NAIC had established a collaborative environment throughout the 2010 MLR implementation process,[96] and noted that the McCarty proposal was "the same proposal that NAHU [the National Association of Health Underwriters] and other agent and broker groups unsuccessfully offered during the NAIC's 2010 deliberations."[97] The letter urged NAIC members to carefully consider how the McCarty proposal could potentially undermine the expected consumer benefits inherent in the ACA's MLR provision.[98]

Specifically, the Chairman's letter pointed out that the ACA's MLR provision was developed and drafted after extensive analysis of the medical loss ratio data submitted by health insurance companies to the NAIC as part of their regular regulatory regime, and both Congress and the Congressional Budget Office relied on data that included in "premiums earned" any and all payments a health insurance company made to an agent or broker related to the sale of a health insurance policy.[99] Chairman Rockefeller argued that excluding agent and broker commissions from the MLR calculation would not only be inconsistent with the health insurance industry's own accounting practices and standards, but would also deprive millions of consumers and business from the rebates and lower premiums they could expect from the MLR provision.[100]

To illustrate how making any changes to agent and broker commissions would have a negative impact on consumers, the letter used data from Maine's request for a MLR waiver.[101] At the time, this kind of detailed data on agent and broker commissions in the individual and group markets was not widely available, but Mega Life & Health Insurance Company (Mega), one of Maine's three major health insurers, was required to disclose it as part of the MLR waiver process. The figure below shows how Mega used its policyholder's premium dollars.

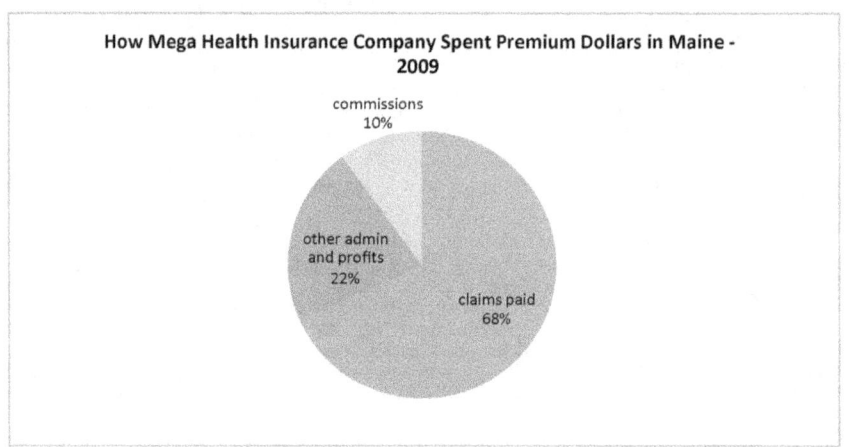

How Mega Health Insurance Company Spent Premium Dollars in Maine - 2009

commissions 10%

other admin and profits 22%

claims paid 68%

[95] Letter from Chairman John D. Rockefeller to Susan E. Voss, President, National Association of Insurance Commissioners (Mar. 15, 2011).

[96] Id. at 2.

[97] Id.

[98] Id. at 3–10.

[99] Id. at 3. Included within the instructions for regulatory filings, the NAIC provided to health insurers the following definition of "written premium": the contractually determined amount charged by the reporting entity [the health insurance company] to the policyholder for the effective period of the contract based on the expectation of risk, policy benefits, and expenses association with the coverage provided by the terms of the contract. Id. at 4.

[100] Id. at 4.

[101] Id. at 6. The ACA allows the Secretary of Health and Human Services to adjust MLR standards for a state if the state can demonstrate that requiring insurers to meet the 80 percent threshold could destabilize the individual market, resulting in fewer choices for consumers. A total of 17 states (ME, NH, NV, KY, FL, GA, ND, IA, LA, KS, DE, IN, MI, TX, OK, NC, WI) have applied for MLR adjustments. Centers for Medicare and Medicaid Services, *State Requests for MLR Adjustment* (online at *http://www.cms.gov/CCIIO/Programs-and-Initiatives/Health-Insurance-Market-Reforms/state_mlr_adj_requests.html*).

In its filing, Mega showed that it used 68 cents out of every dollar on medical expenses and used the remaining 32 cents for administrative costs and profit.[102] Of the 32 cents spent on nonmedical expenses, a full third was spent on paying commissions to agents and brokers.[103] Had Mega been subject to the ACA's MLR provision—with medical premiums of approximately $25 million dollars and a medical loss ratio of 68 percent—it would have owed its almost 14,000 Maine customers a $3 million rebate or about $218 per customer.[104] In contrast, under the McCarty proposal, Mega's $3 million rebate would have decreased to $1 million, denying consumers 66 percent percent of their rebate. According to Chairman Rockefeller, this meant "money that was intended to give consumers relief from the high cost of health care would instead be converted into additional revenue for agents, brokers, and health insurance companies."[105]

The Chairman's final point was to note that agents and brokers earned more revenue when policyholders paid higher premiums and that any reforms like the MLR that sought to decrease what consumers paid in health premiums would also result in decreased income for agents and brokers. With insurance premiums rising at an average annual rate of 6–7 percent over the preceding 10 years, the commission of an insurance agent or broker (in absolute dollars) had roughly doubled.[106] As health insurance companies began the process of reviewing their administrative costs in order to be compliant with the ACA's MLR provision any reductions in health insurance premiums increases would invariably feel like a cut to agents and brokers.[107]

The letter concluded by noting that millions of previously uninsured Americans were soon to be eligible to purchase affordable, comprehensive health care coverage. Although these plans would be offered at lower profit margins, insurance companies, agents, and brokers could expect to see higher sales volume.[108]

b. Spring 2011 NAIC Meeting Austin, Texas

In late March 2011, many of the Nation's insurance commissioners met in Austin, Texas for the NAIC's Spring national meeting. The McCarty proposal was part of the meeting agenda, and at this point encompassed an endorsement of proposed congressional legislation, H.R. 1206, which provided for exclusion of agent and broker fees from the calculation of administrative costs under the MLR formula.[109]

Preceding the meeting, in addition to Chairman Rockefeller's letter, many consumer advocates also voiced concerns regarding the speed with which the NAIC was moving. Ultimately acknowledging these concerns, the NAIC's Professional Health Insurance Advisors Task Force delayed endorsing the McCarty Proposal and instead agreed to further study the issue through its Health and Managed Care Committee.[110] After several weeks of data gathering, the Health and Managed Care Committee delivered its final report ("May Report") to the NAIC on May 26, 2011.[111]

c. May 24, 2011, Committee Majority Staff Report on 2010 MLR Rebates

On May 24, 2011, Chairman Rockefeller issued a Senate Commerce Committee majority staff report ("May 2011 Commerce Committee Report"), marking the first time that estimated savings from the ACA's MLR provision had been quantified using the health insurance companies' own data. Based on preliminary data gathered by the NAIC, the report showed that consumers nationwide would have received almost $2 billion in rebates from their health insurance companies if the

---

[102] Letter from Chairman John D. Rockefeller to Susan E. Voss, President, National Association of Insurance Commissioners, at 6–7 (Mar. 15, 2011).

[103] *Id.* at 7.

[104] *Id.*

[105] *Id.* at 8.

[106] *Id.* at 8–9. The figure applies a 10 percent commission to the average annual premiums for individual health insurance coverage, as presented in, The Kaiser Family Foundation and Health Research & Education Trust, *Employer Health Benefits: 2010 Annual Survey* (Sep. 2, 2010) (online at *http://ehbs.kff.org/pdf/2010/8085.pdf*).

[107] Letter from Chairman John D. Rockefeller to Susan E. Voss, President, National Association of Insurance Commissioners, at 9 (Mar. 15, 2011).

[108] *Id.* at 11.

[109] H.R. 1206, the "Access to Professional Health Insurance Advisors Act of 2011" (112th Congress).

[110] Arthur D. Postal, *NAIC Panel Seeks More Info Before Backing Agent MLR Exemption,* Consumer Watchdog (Mar. 28, 2011).

[111] National Association of Insurance Commissioners, *Report of the Health Care Reform Actuarial (B) Working Group to the Health Insurance and Managed Care (B) Committee on Referral from the Professional Health Insurance Advisors (EX) Task Force Regarding Producer Compensation in the PPACA Medical Loss Ratio Calculation* (May 26, 2011).

MLR provision had been in place for the 2010 reporting year.[112] It also found that more than half of consumers in the individual market would have received rebates in 2010.

The May 2011 Commerce Committee Report also showed that removing agent and broker commissions from the MLR calculation would result in reduced rebates to consumers by more than 60 percent or nearly $1.1 billion.[113] The below table represents the impact of removing agent and broker commissions from the MLR calculation in each market:

Market	Estimated Consumer Rebate Under Current MLR Law ($ millions)	Estimated Consumer Rebate When Commissions are Excluded from MLR Calculation ($ millions)
Individual	$978	$401
Small Group	$447	$146
Large Group	$526	$215
Total	*$1,951*	*$762*

According to the NAIC data reviewed in the majority staff report, if agent and broker commissions had been removed from the MLR calculation in 2010, consumer's rebates would have reduced from $1.95 billion to $762 million.[114] The report also provided a detailed state-by-state breakdown of the rebates consumers would have lost.

The NAIC's Health Insurance Advisors Task Force, using information gathered by the Health and Managed Care Committee, would eventually vote on June 30, 2011, to endorse the proposal to support H.R. 1206, moving consideration to a plenary group of insurance commissioners. On July 12, 2011, Commissioner McCarty brought the H.R. 1206 support proposal before all 50 insurance commissioners for a vote. After California Commissioner Dave Jones and several other commissioners expressed opposition to H.R 1206, the NAIC ultimately did not hold a plenary vote on the proposal.[115] Although tabled for a time, the McCarty proposal would reappear at the NAIC's 2011 Fall National Meeting in Washington D.C.

d. November 21, 2011, Letter from Chairman Rockefeller to Commissioner Kevin McCarty

Just prior to the NAIC's Fall 2011 meeting, Chairman Rockefeller wrote to Commissioner McCarty reiterating that removal of agent and broker commissions from the MLR calculation would be contrary to congressional intent. The Chairman's letter pointed out that the NAIC's own report found that "a significant number of companies have not reduced commissions in 2011."[116] Further, based on review of new data HHS had obtained from states submitting MLR waiver requests, the letter analyzed the negative impact removing agent and broker commissions would have in a number of states. The letter noted that while Kentucky, Georgia, and Delaware all claimed that the MLR was causing significant disruptions within their agent and broker communities, "[t]o date, HHS has not yet found any convincing evidence that 'consumers may be unable to access agents and brokers' under the minimum [MLR] law."[117] In fact, in Kentucky, agent and broker commissions had actually increased; Georgia saw no decreases; and only one of nine insurers in Delaware decreased commissions.[118]

Chairman Rockefeller stressed that while the early effects of the law had shown that consumers continued to enjoy access to the services of agents and brokers, any changes to the MLR's treatment of agent and broker commissions would have a negative impact on consumers. Using information from the NAIC's May Report, the letter discussed the impact removing agent and broker commission would have for Florida's health insurance consumers. The below chart demonstrates this distinction:

---

[112] Senate Committee on Commerce, Science, and Transportation, *Majority Staff Report on Consumer Health Insurance Savings Under the Medical Loss Ratio Law,* at 1 (May 24, 2011).
  [113] *Id.*
  [114] *Id.* at 4.
  [115] Arthur D. Postal, *PPACA: NAIC Ices Agent Comp MLR Exclusion Effort,* LifeHealthPro (July 12, 2011) (online at *http://www.lifehealthpro.com/2011/07/12/ppaca-naic-ices-agent-comp-mlr-exclusion-effort*).
  [116] Letter from Chairman John D. Rockefeller to Kevin McCarty, President-Elect, National Association of Insurance Commissioners, at 2 (Nov. 21, 2011).
  [117] *Id.* at 3.
  [118] *Id.* at 3–4.

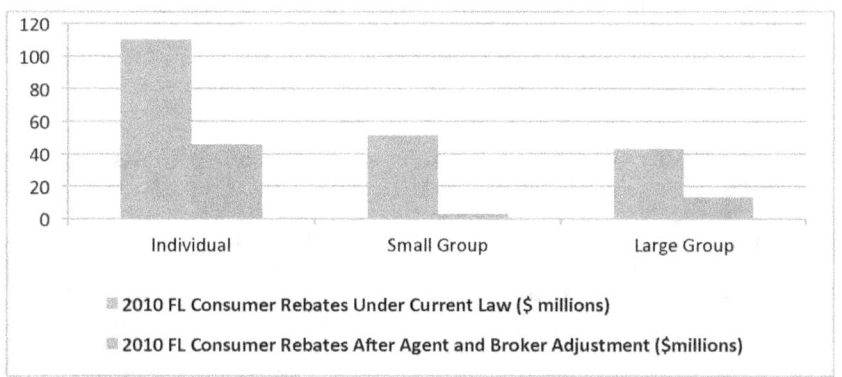

If agent and broker commissions were eliminated from the MLR, Florida consumers would have lost $142 million or over 60 percent of the estimated $200 million they would have received in rebates if the law had been in effect in 2010. Under the McCarty proposal, consumers would have lost not just hundreds of millions of dollars in annual rebates, but "health insurance companies [would] lose the incentive the current law gives them to run their businesses more efficiently and deliver a better value to their customers at a lower cost." [119] The Chairman emphasized his strong support of the agent and broker community, and at the same time reiterated that any changes to the MLR could not diminish the value of the expected consumer benefits.

e. NAIC Endorses Modified McCarty Resolution

On November 22, 2011, Commissioner McCarty introduced a modified agents and brokers resolution before a plenary of NAIC insurance commissioners. Instead of fully endorsing H.R. 1206, the resolution urged HHS to exempt agent and broker commissions from the MLR calculation and for HHS to place a hold on MLR implementation in order for state waiver requests to be filed. The resolution passed 26–20 after a 90-minute debate—and two unsuccessful attempts by insurance commissioners to modify the resolutions language.[120] Many insurance commissioners expressed concerns with the resolution. Commissioner Sandy Praeger, a Republican from Kansas, voiced concern about the future credibility of the NAIC saying, "we [NAIC] were written into the [PPACA] law because we were trusted as experts on this. We are going so far here as to put our credibility in jeopardy." [121]

Ultimately H.R. 1206, although reported out of the House Energy and Commerce Committee, failed to secure a vote on the House floor and died at the end of the 112th Congressional session.[122]

III. Conclusion

Prior to health reform, for-profit health insurers carefully tracked their medical loss ratios and worked to lower them. A low MLR was a signal to investors that an insurer was spending less on health care and had more potential money for shareholders. The inclusion of minimum MLR requirements in health reform changed this dynamic. By setting a floor on health insurer expenditures of premium dollars for consumer medical care, the law prevents for-profit insurers from relentlessly cutting medical expenditures to boost profits.

Today, the medical loss ratio provisions of the health reform law have already proved to be a significant success story for American consumers. In the four years since enactment of health reform, individuals and small businesses across the country have seen billions of dollars of savings due to the MLR requirements, including $1.6 billion in rebates and hundreds of millions of more due to improved insurer efficiencies. At the same time the MLR public reporting requirements have opened a new window into the operations of the insurance industry, helping consumers

---

[119] *Id.* at 5.

[120] Elizabeth D. Festa, *NAIC Narrowly Passes Resolution Urging HHS to Exempt Agent Commissions from PPACA* Standard, LifeHealthPro (Nov. 22, 2011) (online at *http://www.life healthpro.com/2011/11/22/naic-narrowly-passes-resolution-urging-hhs-to-exem?page=3*).

[121] *Id.*

[122] H.R. 1206, 112th Cong. (2012).

compare and choose products, and providing new data to help policy experts, financial analysts, and others evaluate industry trends.

Looking forward, the MLR requirements will serve as permanent incentives for the insurance industry to operate with efficiency and transparency, and to make sure consumers receive appropriate value for their premium dollars.

The CHAIRMAN. Now, that the dust has settled and the data is in, it is hard to see what all the fuss was about. Health insurers who have not met the 80 percent threshold have cut rebate checks totaling almost $2 billion to their customers. That is very good news. But the even better news is what people do not think of, and that is that the law forced insurance companies to review their operations and reduce their non-healthcare related costs, and they are doing that. Rebate amounts are, therefore, dropping, and there is a very simple reason for that, because health insurance companies increased their efficiency and the quality of their products. That cost cutting, by the way, has saved consumers hundreds of millions of dollars more.

The minimum medical loss ratio is a very simple idea, but it appears to have had a powerful and very positive effect on the health insurance market. Consumers are getting a better deal than they were getting 5 years. I look forward to talking about how and why this worked in the commercial market, and whether we can apply it to other parts of our healthcare sectors, such as Medicaid managed care.

And that is the end of me, and I now present to you my good friend and distinguished Ranking Member, John Thune, whose brother is about to be here.

Senator THUNE. He is here. Right there.

The CHAIRMAN. And so, you are Bob. Bob, I want to tell you, begging sufferance from membership, that you have a superb brother. He may be younger than you. And you gone into a profession which he indicates that your mother probably prefers that he had gone into. But I would argue that because I would say he is a superb legislator and a superb senator. I am a Democrat, he is a Republican. It makes absolutely no difference whatsoever. We get a lot done together. So the Thune family, wherever they are at this very moment, should be very proud of both of you.

STATEMENT OF HON. JOHN THUNE, U.S. SENATOR FROM SOUTH DAKOTA

Senator THUNE. Thank you, Mr. Chairman. My gosh. How can I not say good things about Obamacare now after you do that? I appreciate that. It is nice to have my brother here. He is older, by 15 years. He still has all his hair, which is something that some of us who are losing are a little chagrined about.

The CHAIRMAN. I would not worry.

Senator THUNE. Thank you. But I appreciate you having the hearing, Mr. Chairman, and your diligent work on one particular issue of the healthcare law, which I think you have given a tremendous amount of attention to. And I know we are going to talk a lot about that and hear from our panelists here today. I want to talk, too, in the broader context about the Affordable Care Act.

But as we do think about the law and its impact across the country, I want to underscore a quote from a constituent of mine, Dale, who wrote to me saying, and I quote, "I feel the Federal Government has stolen over $5,000 [per year] from me." He is referring to the significant premium increase, as well as a jump in his deductible, under Obamacare.

Another constituent from South Dakota, Roxanne, received a quote of $400 more per month, or $4,000 more per year, under Obamacare than her current health insurance plan. With two kids to get through college, Roxanne and her husband cannot afford a total monthly health insurance payment that is more than their mortgage payment on a monthly basis. So she wrote to me and said, and I quote, "Please do something about this. There has to be a better way."

So those are just a couple of the continuing frustrations that I hear from people in South Dakota when it comes to some of the negative impacts of the Affordable Care Act, otherwise known as Obamacare. Now, thankfully Dale and Roxanne believe in a representative democracy that laws can be changed or repealed, so they along with many others have shared their stories about the damaging impacts of this law.

The idea of the medical loss ratio provision in the Affordable Care Act, which has been championed, as I said, by the Chairman, requires insurers to spend the majority of premium dollars on efforts to improve healthcare quality, and it places a cap on administrative costs. Consumers can benefit under this provision by gaining greater transparency as to how insurers spend premium dollars, and in some cases, getting a rebate from insurers that miss the MLR target.

In 2012, the average rebate per family in South Dakota was $70 for the approximately 700 million individuals who received a rebate, or just about $5 a month. This is also roughly the same amount of the previous year's average rebate in my home state. Now, I know there are other states that have had different experiences, have seen higher rebates than South Dakota, but I think it is important to keep the issue in perspective: approximately 500 million, in MLR rebates were paid out nationwide in 2012, a figure that is likely to decline for 2013.

At the same time, recent news accounts show that nearly the same amount was squandered on the failed health exchanges in just four states, and hundreds of millions have been wasted on contractors who have been paid to sit idle in Obamacare processing centers. It is hard to see this as a net gain for consumers and taxpayers.

I appreciate the Chairman's dedication to protecting consumers and the MLR provision. It is well intentioned. We all want quality healthcare and affordable insurance premiums, but I worry that the MLR provision and the healthcare law as a whole are having negative consequences on insured individuals and the many Americans who are frustrated that promises about how the legislation was going to work have proven to be untrue.

The intent of the MLR is to help contain spending on health insurance, which is a laudable goal. But some experts believe that the MLR could actually increase the cost of premiums and narrow the competition in the marketplace. I am also concerned that the MLR regulation put forth by HHS can undermine efforts by insurers to prevent fraud and abuse, including efforts to prevent the delivery of inappropriate or unnecessary services that may harm consumers.

Even if the MLR could be implemented without those consequences, we cannot ignore the law's larger negative impact. How do consumers benefit when the cost of other Obamacare provisions exceed any potential benefits that they would get from the MLR. As just one example, according to a summation compiled by the House Ways and Means Committee regarding estimates from the non-partisan Joint Committee on Taxation and the CBO, tax increases from Obamacare are estimated to total $1 trillion over 10 years. Some of those costs are going to be passed on directly to consumers, including my constituents in South Dakota and many other Americans.

Taken as a whole, Obamacare continues to wreak havoc on our economy and on job creation. More and more Americans are losing their existing healthcare, and as a result of the employer mandate, businesses are cutting hours to reduce the number of full-time employees on their books. Ultimately, the Congressional Budget Office estimates that due to the decline in hours worked, Obamacare will result in losses equal to two and a half million fewer full-time workers.

I want to reiterate what Roxanne wrote to me—"There has to be a better way." Consumers should get appropriate value for their premium dollars on health insurance, and the MLR is a well-intentioned attempt at achieving that. But when one steps back to look at the larger picture, it is increasingly evident that the many problematic costs in regulations associated with the healthcare law will almost certainly frustrate that purpose.

Mr. Chairman, I want to thank you again for holding this hearing. I look forward to hearing from our witnesses on this particular subject. And again, credit your hard work on this element of Obamacare, and wish that I could speak more favorably about other elements of the bill.

Thank you, Mr. Chairman.

The CHAIRMAN. Thank you, Senator Thune. Incidentally, does everybody have a copy of this? Do you? OK. Because this is just like anything else. I mean, this is like the Intelligence Committee when we are going after the intelligence community, you write reports. But you always include a lot of reference notes, in other words, because if you have reference notes, that means that you can go right back to the person, or to the e-mail, or to the telephone call, whatever. In other words, it talks about the accuracy of the report.

Before I begin—no. First, we are going to do it properly. We are going to go to Mr. Wendell Potter. Any time you do that, you are doing something useful and good for the country. And Wendell and I sort of fell into a great friendship when he had the unbelievable courage to step forward and for the first to open the chest cavity of insurance company practices and did so forthrightly, has written books on it, always in a very even voice without undue attacks or anything else. He just tells it as he sees it.

So Wendell Potter is an Analyst for the Center for Public Integrity and a former Health Insurance Executive for Cigna. Mr. Mark Hall, Professor of Law, from Wake Forest, and Mr. Jack Ralston.

I am going to say something about him because he could not come. Ms. Katherine Fernandez of Houston, Texas. That is you. And Mrs. Grace-Marie Turner, President of the Galen Institute.

Can I just, Wendell, before you start, say that what John Ralston was going to say, we will make a part of the record obviously.

[The information referred to follows:]

PREPARED STATEMENT OF JOHN RALSTON, HAMPTON, VIRGINIA

Chairman Rockefeller, Ranking Member Thune, and members of the Committee. I want to thank you for inviting me here today. My name is John Ralston, and I'm President of Bihrle Applied Research located in Hampton, Virginia. The costs of healthcare have had a significant impact on the financial well-being of my company. I greatly appreciate the opportunity to present my perspective.

Bihrle Applied Research is a technology company located in the Hampton Roads area of Virginia that is involved in the aircraft testing, flight control and simulation development aspects of both civil and military aviation. We've been in business for over 40 years and have worked with most of the world's major and minor aircraft manufacturers, as well as a majority of the world's governmental authorities associated with aviation. We have a talented and motivated staff, and finding and keeping these sorts of people require, among other things, a health care plan that is at least competitive with other major companies. Being a small company of 26 engineers and software developers means that we have limited and somewhat more expensive choices in this regard. In the earlier years of the company's history, our health coverage consisted of an expensive plan from a major provider that had high deductibles, such that most of our people rarely received any contribution from the provider for any of their health care. Obviously, this was unpopular and after becoming president, I examined our options in more detail. We were able to find a PPO plan with the MAMSI health insurance company that had $10 copays for most doctor visits and drugs, and while the selection of plan doctors was adequate, they also paid 80 percent of off-plan visits. We also added, for the first time in the company history, a very limited dental plan, one that provided limited coverage for dentist visits, fillings and x-rays, but nothing for more serious dental work. This was a significant upgrade in the Bihrle Applied Research's healthcare at the time, and was very nearly the same cost as our previous plan, with the company at the time paying the entire cost of the healthcare. This health insurance company was eventually bought by United Healthcare, and over the years the cost for family coverage has gradually increased from approximately $370 permonth in the late 1990s to over $2,000 per month today. Heath care of the employees is essentially our largest expense besides salaries, over $300,000 per year for a staff of 26, essentially equivalent to the company's total tax bill. As the costs have escalated over the years, we've introduced a number of options for the employees including the company fully paying for an HMO plan and allowing employees to pay the difference for varying levels of PPO plans. Since everyone has eventually opted for the PPO plans, our current approach pays 85 percent of the total cost for the least of two PPO plans. Most employees select the highest plan and pay the monthly difference.

Because of the dominance of health care costs in the company's finances, we watched the progress of the ACA with concern as to the impacts on coverage and cost. At the outset of the program, the first thing that we noticed was no significant change in the rate of increase of the program cost. Obviously, for the cost per family to go from $368 per month to over $2,000 per month, there had been double digit percentages of increase nearly every year since we first established the program. At this point, the increases, while still objectionable, have stayed consistent with previous years; with 2013 percent increase dropping slightly. The most welcome effect has been the impact of the Medical Loss Ratio component of the ACA which, for us, has resulted in refunds of $5,000 and $6,000 over the last two years. With the availability of this rebate, the decision was made to use this money to improve the coverage of the dental plan. This rebate obviously did not cover the complete amount of the increase, but was enough that the remaining contribution for the company was acceptable. The upgraded dental policy now covers more serious dental work and surgery, including, root canals, crown and implants. In the past two years, this coverage has been of significant benefit to many of the company employees, my self included, where I personally was able to save over $2500 on a recent implant. The overall satisfaction with the company's health coverage is the highest it has ever been in my 33 year history with the company.

The epilogue to this story is that we remain hopeful that we will continue getting the rebate, primarily because we have a healthy staff that is conscious of their health, so our overall claims have been relatively low. Health maintenance is something the company encourages by allowing employees flexible hours for exercise time during the workday, as well as other support for gym memberships. Nevertheless, healthcare costs continue to escalate, and at some point we may have to transfer more cost to the employees. We are hopeful that the rate of increase will continue to slow. The fact remains that health care is effectively our largest non-salary cost, and when we compare the total of our tax and health care costs, we are still at a disadvantage to European competitors, with their higher taxes, but absence of company funded health care costs.

The CHAIRMAN. But when he got into this, I think he was a little skeptical at first. But he said that since this thing went into effect, the percent increase in the cost of coverage for his employees declined slightly in 2013 from previous years. The company received medical loss ratio refunds of $5,000 to $6,000 over the last 2 years. This rebate money he put to work improving the dental plan that the company provides, which Mr. Ralston said has been of significant benefit to many of the company's employees. So he is pleased.

And I am pleased to introduce Wendell Potter.

STATEMENT OF WENDELL POTTER, ANALYST, CENTER FOR PUBLIC INTEGRITY AND FORMER HEALTH INSURANCE EXECUTIVE

Mr. POTTER. Mr. Chairman, Ranking Member Thune, and members of the Committee, thank you for the opportunity to be here this afternoon. I also want to thank you, Mr. Chairman, for your tireless efforts to ensure that the Affordable Care Act contains language to address what had been a steady decrease in the medical loss ratio over more than a decade. As a result of the MLR provision in the law, Americans with private health insurance have saved billions of dollars that otherwise would have gone to unnecessary overhead and excess profits.

It has been almost 5 years since I first appeared before this committee and spoke about the medical loss ratio, which was then an obscure term that was known by few other than insurance company executives, Wall Street financial analysts, and shareholders. As I said then, the average family had almost no understanding of how influential Wall Street has become and the decisions made by insurance company executives about how much of policyholders' premiums would actually be used to pay for medical care.

I noted that financial analysts and shareholders of publicly-traded health insurers are as interested in a medical loss ratio as they are in earnings per share. To win the favor of influential analysts, executives of four private insurers had to demonstrate during every quarter every quarterly earnings call that their companies made more during the most recent quarter than a year earlier, and that the portion of the premium going to pay for medical care, or the MLR, was declining. If they had to acknowledge that the company had to spend a slightly higher percentage of premiums on medical claims than anticipated, they knew that some of their investors would be disappointed enough to sell their shares, which would inevitably result in a drop in the stock price and the value of the company.

During my last 10 years as an industry executive, one of my main responsibilities was to handle financial communications to the media. In preparing for quarterly earnings reports, the first numbers that I looked for were the earnings per share in the medical loss ratio. I could predict with some certainty whether the company's stock price would go up or down the day we announced quarterly earnings by looking at just those numbers. I once saw a competitor's stock price drop 20 percent—20 percent—in a single day when the company reported that its MLR for the quarter had increased by just one and a half percent.

In my previous testimony, I detailed some of the actions insurers took to reduce the chances that analysts and investors would be disappointed, including dumping policyholders when they got sick. By requiring insurers to spend at least 80 percent of what policyholders pay in premiums on medical claims or to improve the quality of care they receive, as the Affordable Care Act does, the influence of Wall Street has been reduced.

As you know, a primary goal of the MLR requirements in the ACA was to help consumers realize fuller value of their health insurance payments. Since those requirements went into effect in 2011, that goal has indeed been realized.

Consumers benefit from the MLR requirements in two significant ways. First, insurers are now operating more cost efficiently to stay in compliance with the law. As a result, many policyholders are paying lower premiums than they would have been charged otherwise. Second, if an insurer fails to comply and spends less than 80 percent on medical care or 85 percent in the large group market, it has to issue rebates to its policyholders.

Individuals and families who are not able to get coverage through an employer have seen the greatest benefit. According to the Kaiser Family Foundation, the average MLR in the individual market increases from 78 percent in 2010 to 83 percent in 2012. Researchers at the Foundation estimated that had it not been for the MLR requirements in the ACA, premiums in the individual market would have been almost $900 million higher in 2011, and nearly $2 billion higher in 2012.

As you may know, I had the privilege of serving as a consumer representative to the National Association of Insurance Commissioners when that organization was working in 2010 to draft the MLR regulations. The insurance industry flooded the Commissioners with comment letters as part of an intense lobbying effort to persuade the NAIC to give insurers broad latitude to comply with the law. They argued that many of the activities they had always categorized as administrative in nature should be counted among quality improvement expenses.

Despite being outspent and out-lobbied by what could be considered an order of magnitude, the NAIC's consumer representatives were successful in pushing back against the industry. Most of the industry's requests were rejected by the Commissioners as being unreasonable and contrary to the intent of the law.

The MLR requirements ensure that consumers can now have greater confidence in knowing that most of what they pay in premiums will be used to pay for medical care or to improve the quality of care, and that no more than 20 percent of their premiums will go to unnecessary overhead or to reward insurance company executives and shareholders. Overall, the 80/20 rule has had a positive impact on the pocketbooks of millions of consumers, and it will continue to help ensure that Americans can realize the full value of their health insurance payments.

Thank you.

[The prepared statement of Mr. Potter follows:]

PREPARED STATEMENT OF WENDELL POTTER, PHILADELPHIA, PA

Mr. Chairman, Ranking Member Thune and members of the Committee, thank you for the opportunity to be here this afternoon.

I also want to thank you, Mr. Chairman, for your tireless efforts to ensure that the Affordable Care Act contained language to address what had been a steady decrease in the medical loss ratio (MLR) over more than a decade. As a result of the MLR provision in the law, Americans with private health insurance have saved billions of dollars that otherwise would have gone to unnecessary overhead and excess profits.

It has been almost five years since I first appeared before this committee and spoke about the medical loss ratio, which was then an obscure term known by few other than insurance company executives, Wall Street financial analysts and shareholders. As I said then, the average family had almost no understanding of how influential Wall Street had become in the decisions made by insurance company executives about how much of policyholders' premiums would actually be used to pay medical claims.

I noted that financial analysts and shareholders of publicly traded health insurers are as interested in the medical loss ratio as they are in earnings per share. To win the favor of influential analysts, executives of for-profit insurers had to demonstrate during every quarterly earnings call that their companies made more money during the most recent quarter than a year earlier and that the portion of the premium going to pay medical claims—the MLR—was declining. If they had to acknowledge that the company had to spend a slightly higher percentage of premiums on medical claims than anticipated, they knew that some of their investors would be disappointed enough to sell their shares, which would inevitably result in a drop in the stock price and the value of the company.

During my last 10 years as an industry executive, one of my main responsibilities was to handle financial communications to the media. In preparing for quarterly earnings reports, the first numbers I looked for were the earnings per share and the medical loss ratio. I could predict with some certainty whether the company's stock price would go up or down the day we announced quarterly earnings by looking at just those two numbers. I once saw a competitor's stock price drop 20 percent in a single day when the company reported that its MLR for the quarter had increased by just one and a half percent.

A study conducted by PriceWaterhouseCoopers in 2008 showed how successful executives at publicly traded companies had been in reducing the percentage of premium revenue on medical care. The accounting firm found that the medical loss ratios of the seven largest for-profit insurers fell from an average of 85.3 percent in 1998 to 81.6 percent in 2008. By reducing the MLR 3.7 percent over those years, the insurance companies avoided paying out billions of dollars for medical care and were able to use that money to reward executives and shareholders—at the obvious expense of their policyholders.

In my previous testimony, I detailed some of the actions insurers took to reduce the chances that analysts and investors would be disappointed, including dumping policyholders when they got sick. By requiring insurers to spend at least 80 percent of what policyholders pay in premiums on medical claims or to improve the quality of care they receive, as the Affordable Care Act does, the influence of Wall Street has been reduced.

As you know, a primary goal of the MLR requirements in the ACA was to help consumers realize fuller value of their health insurance payments. Since those requirements went into effect in 2011, that goal has indeed been realized.

Consumers benefit from the MLR requirements in two significant ways. First, insurers are now operating more cost-efficiently to stay in compliance with the law. As a result, many policyholders are paying lower premiums than they would have been charged otherwise. Second, if an insurer fails to comply and spends less than 80 percent on medical care—or 85 percent in the large group market—it has to issue rebates to its policyholders.

Individuals and families who are not able to get coverage through an employer have seen the greatest benefit. According to the Kaiser Family Foundation, the average MLR in the individual market increased from 78 percent in 2010 to 83 percent in 2012. Researchers at the Foundation estimated that had it not been for the MLR requirements in the ACA, premiums in the individual market would have been $856 million higher in 2011 and $1.9 billion higher in 2012.

During my two decades in the insurance industry, my colleagues and I never tired of saying that steps needed to be taken to remove costs from the U.S. health care system. Although the industry spent considerable time and resources lobbying against the MLR requirements—and later to try to shape the regulations pertaining to the requirements—the 80/20 rule, as it is often called, has done what the industry said was needed. During the first two years that the rule has been in effect, according to a report published earlier this month by the Commonwealth Fund, at least $3 billion in costs were removed from our health care system, with American consumers being the beneficiary.

Approximately half of those savings were in the form or rebates: $1.1 billion in 2011 and $513 million in 2012. Insurers sent out fewer rebate checks in 2012 than in 2011 because most of them quickly implemented the changes necessary to stay in compliance with the law. Had the MLR requirement been in effect in 2010, by the way, consumers across all the market segments would have received close to $2 billion in rebates, according to the Commonwealth Fund. Imagine how much consumers would have saved if the requirement had been in effect during earlier years.

The other way consumers have benefited is the reduction in overhead in the insurance industry. The Commonwealth Fund calculated that $1.75 billion in overhead was eliminated during the first two years alone. Most of those savings came in 2012 as health insurers continued to reduce their administrative and sales costs, such as brokers' fees, without increasing their profit margins.

It's important to note that although broker commissions decreased by almost $300 million across all market segments in 2012, that represented only about 3.5 percent of total broker expense that year.

As you may know, I had the privilege of serving as a consumer representative to the National Association of Insurance Commissioners when that organization was working in 2010 to draft the MLR regulations. The insurance industry flooded the commissioners with comment letters as part of an intense lobbying effort to persuade the NAIC to give insurers broad latitude to comply with the law. They argued that many of the activities they had always categorized as administrative in nature—such as their spending to reduce fraud and to meet accreditation requirements—should be counted among quality improvement expenses. And lobbyists for insurers and brokers joined forces in an intense campaign to get broker fees exempted from the MLR equation. Despite being outspent and out-lobbied by what could be considered an order of magnitude, the NAIC's consumer representatives were successful in pushing back against the industry. Most of the industry's requests were rejected by the commissioners as being unreasonable and contrary to the intent of the law.

It's worth noting that some critics predicted that the MLR requirements would result in a mass exodus of insurers from the marketplace. That has not happened. In fact, insurers have continued to do quite well financially since the MLR rules went into effect. According to an analysis by the Commonwealth Fund, insurers' total profits for all markets have declined by only 0.1 percent of premiums.

Another benefit of the MLR requirements to consumers as well as to policymakers and regulators is the enhanced transparency they have brought to the insurance industry. We now have much better insights into how insurers spend the premiums they collect from policyholders as a result of the additional reporting requirements.

We have learned, for example, that nonprofit insurers have done a much better job of complying with the 80/20 rule than their for-profit competitors. As Commonwealth Fund researchers noted in a report last year, publicly traded insurers appear to aim their pricing closer to the minimum loss ratio, no doubt because that is what Wall Street demands they do. Their adjusted MLR marketwide has been "virtually identical" to the 80 percent limit.

The researchers found that only eight percent of nonprofit insurers owed a rebate in the individual market in 2011 compared with 47 percent of for-profit insurers. Additionally, the average amount of the rebates owed by the nonprofits were considerably lower than those owed by the for-profits.

Still, all consumers, whether enrolled in a plan operated by a nonprofit or for-profit company, continue to benefit from what has become one of the most important cost-saving provisions of the Affordable Care Act.

The MLR requirements ensure that consumers can now have greater confidence in knowing that most of what they pay in premiums will be used to pay for medical care or improve the quality of that care, and that no more than 20 percent of their premiums will go to unnecessary overhead or to reward insurance company executives and shareholders.

Overall, the 80/20 rule has had a very positive impact on the pocketbooks of millions of consumers, and it will continue to help ensure that Americans can realize the full value of their health insurance payments.

Thank you.

The CHAIRMAN. Thank you, sir, very much.

Mr. Mark Hall, Professor of Law, Wake Forest University.

STATEMENT OF MARK A. HALL, PROFESSOR OF LAW AND PUBLIC HEALTH, WAKE FOREST UNIVERSITY

Mr. HALL. Chairman Rockefeller, Ranking Member Thune, and distinguished members of this committee, it is a true honor to speak before you about the work that Dr. Michael McCue and I have done, who is with us here from Virginia Commonwealth University, over the last few years analyzing data regarding the medical loss ratio and reported in a series of publications issued by the Commonwealth Fund, and published with Health Affairs.

I will briefly make three sets of remarks, the first speaking to the primary consumer benefits from the 80/20 rule, amplifying some of what Mr. Potter said. Second, talking about some of the secondary beneficiaries or potential drawbacks of the rule, and third, thinking very briefly about possibilities for expanding or improving the rule.

I think one of the remarkable things about the Federal MLR rule is this transformation of the MLR from a measure of keen consumer interest that Mr. Potter described under which a lower medical loss ratio was better. The whole concept of medical loss emphasizes that from an investor's point of view, it was a bad thing to pay medical claims. And now, the MLR has been turned 180 degrees in the other direction, viewing it as an indicator of consumer value in which a higher MLR is better for consumers because this means that the premium dollars are being used more effectively to provide benefits, and perhaps it should be renamed the medical benefit ratio instead of the medical loss ratio to signify this remarkable transformation of the indicator of consumer value rather than a potential for investor profits.

Now, that said, it is not the perfect measure of all things of consumer value. There are certainly things—aspects of administrative expenses that bring consumer value, such as some part of administrative expenses go to attempting to lower claims cost and, therefore, producing lower premiums. Also paying some of the sales costs helps to educate consumers in terms of their options and help them make the best choices. And these things count on the negative side of the equation.

This is not to mean that they provide no value, but that the key value that people look for in insurance is providing and paying for medical care. And so, it is not the perfect measure or the sole measure for consumer value, but it is certainly a very good measure, and one that has been brought much more to prominence as a result of this Federal rule.

Obviously the direct rebates are the most direct indicator of consumer value, and the $1.6 billion that has been awarded over the first 2 years is quite substantial. This year's rebates will not be announced until August, I believe, and we will see whether the numbers continue at that level or drop down. But as the Chairman noted, the fact that the rebates may diminish does not undercut the second set of direct consumer benefits from the MLR rule, which is simply that under the spotlight of regulatory oversight, insurers are induced to make their products more efficient by reducing their administrative costs and profits, their non-medical overhead.

And that reduction so far has been at least as significant as the rebates. The work Dr. McCue and I have done indicates something like one and three-quarter billion dollars reduction in non-medical overhead over the first two years. Others have indicated as much as a $3 billion reduction in overhead.

And it is not simply the size of these numbers, but the fact that—I use the analogy that it is like a dieter who loses weight. You have the benefit of that during the first year, but it is the sort of consumer gift that keeps on giving. As long as those reduced, sort of leaner, products, leaner overhead, remains in place year after year, consumers receive the benefit of that even if it does not grow larger.

Now, considering some of the possible drawbacks, as the Chairman noted, a vast set of dire consequences were predicted, but these really have not been experienced at all. To the contrary, the insurance industry looks quite strong judged by the stock market. Stock prices have gone up considerably more than the market wide averages since the MLR rule went into effect, reflecting not only the lack of its harming the industry, but also the Affordable Care Act as a whole.

Nor have we seen this exodus of insurers that was predicted from the regulated market. The notion that their profits might be regulated led a number of insurers to say, you know, we are going to leave the market. There has been some contraction, but it is more or less in line with the contraction we have seen in the industry as a whole over the last few years. And we still have roughly 500 insurers in each significant market segment throughout the country. And insurers in particular are entering the individual market, which is the market that was the most directly affected by the MLR rule, so certainly no indication there of any harms.

Regarding potential changes to the rule, from where I sit the rule seems to be working well. It could obviously always be improved or tweaked in various ways. But the one area that is not addressed by the MLR rule is Medicaid managed care companies, private insurers that provide through Medicaid. And states do have some oversight of the MLRs for Medicaid managed care companies, but as the situation was before, the Federal rule for commercial insurers, as the Chairman noted, the rules are not uniform, and they are not comprehensive across the country.

So that is an area where I do not have a position staked out, but it is certainly worth more investigation for whether perhaps some of the benefits, not just in terms of setting a minimum, but also standardization and transparency all following the same rule and all being sort of clear what the rule is and how well it is being met, I think are benefits—secondary benefits that we have seen that could well extend to other areas of healthcare spending.

So thank you for your time, and I would be happy to answer questions.

[The prepared statement of Mr. Hall follows:]

PREPARED STATEMENT OF MARK A. HALL, PROFESSOR OF LAW AND PUBLIC HEALTH, WAKE FOREST UNIVERSITY AND MICHAEL J. MCCUE, PROFESSOR OF HEALTH ADMINISTRATION, VIRGINIA COMMONWEALTH UNIVERSITY

Chairman Rockefeller, Ranking Member Thune, and distinguished Members of the Committee, thank you for the opportunity to testify today about the Federal regulation of health insurers' medical loss ratios (MLRs). This is a topic that my colleague, Dr. Michael McCue at Virginia Commonwealth, and I have studied in depth for the past two years as reported in a series of publications with the Commonwealth Fund.[1]

I will divide my remarks into three parts: (1) the primary consumer benefits from the Affordable Care Act's (ACA's) MLR rule; (2) secondary benefits or harms from this rule; and (3) opportunities for expanding or improving the rule.

Direct Consumer Benefits

Traditionally, the MLR has been used mainly as an indicator of financial strength. For investors or lenders, a lower MLR is more favorable because it signals the potential for higher profits. The ACA's MLR rule has reversed this directional field—focusing on the MLR as a measure of consumer value. For consumers, a higher MLR is more favorable because this means that a greater portion of the premium dollar is going to pay for medical treatment and quality improvement activities rather than for sales expenses, administrative overhead, or profits. The MLR is not a perfect measure for consumer value; some portion of administrative expense is used to reduce medical costs, which can bring consumer value by reducing total premium costs. No performance measure is perfect. But, despite its limitations, the MLR is a very useful measure of efficiency and consumer value.

Under the ACA, the most direct consumer benefit from a minimum medical loss ratio is to require health insurers to rebate to consumer any amounts by which they fall short of the minimum. Thus, in the individual or small group markets, where the minimum MLR is 80 percent, if an individual insurer spends only 75 percent of its premium dollars on medical claims and quality improvement expenses in a year, it must rebate five percent of its premiums to subscribers after year-end accounting. The minimum MLR for large groups is 85 percent, reflecting the greater economies of scale in that market segment.

The ACA's MLR rule took effect in 2011. For that year, health insurers rebated $1.1 billion to consumers. In 2012, rebates dropped in half, to $513 million, indicating greater compliance with the minimum MLRs. Rebates for 2013 will be determined by August of this year.

Consumer benefits from MLR regulation are not restricted to rebates, however. To avoid having to pay rebates, insurers can increase their MLRs by reducing overhead expenses and profits. Doing that makes insurance a better value for consumers. In fact, insurers have done just this in the first two years under the ACA's MLR rule.[2] In 2011, the first year under the MLR rule, health insurers reduced overall profits and administrative costs by $350 million. Changes in financial performance were most apparent in the individual market, where the median medical loss ratio increased by 5.5 percentage points from 2010 to 2011. The median administrative cost ratio declined by 2.6 percentage points, and the median operating margin declined by 1.3 percentage points. Within the individual market, such changes were most notable among for-profit insurers. These insurers raised their median medical loss ratio from 72 percent in 2010 to 79 percent in 2011—much closer to

---

[1] M. J. McCue and M. A. Hall, The Federal Medical Loss Ratio Rule: Implications for Consumers in Year 2, The Commonwealth Fund, May 2014

M. McCue, M. Hall, and X. Liu, "Impact of Medical Loss Regulation on the Financial Performance of Health Insurers," Health Affairs, Sept. 2013 32(9):1546–51.

Mark A. Hall and Michael J. McCue, Insurers' Medical Loss Ratios and Quality Improvement Spending in 2011, The Commonwealth Fund, March 2013.

M. J. McCue and M. A. Hall, Insurers' Responses to Regulation of Medical Loss Ratios, The Commonwealth Fund, December 2012.

[2] It is not accurate to attribute all such changes to the MLR rule, but the closer in time that overhead reductions are to the new MLR rule, the more likely the rule played a major role in encouraging any increase in health insurers' efficiency.

the required minimum level. In 2012, insurers continued to reduce their administrative and sales costs and their profit margins, by $1.4 billion overall.

It is not known exactly how much of the reduced overhead these two years can be attributed to the new MLR regulation rather than market competition. But, it seems reasonable to estimate that, in the first two years under this regulation, total consumer benefits related to the MLR regulation—both in rebates and reduced overhead—amounted to over $3 billion. It is also important to note that, unlike rebates that are paid in a single year, a one-year reduction in overhead pays consumer dividends year after year, as long as the reduction is maintained. Therefore, even if MLR rebates diminish even further, consumers will still continue to receive the benefits of reduced overhead year after year, relative to what it would have been without the improvement in the MLR.

Secondary Benefits or Harms

Another important benefit of the Federal MLR rule is simply the transparency and standardization it provides for those who study or observe health insurers' financial performance and consumer value. Prior to the ACA, insurers did not consistently report their MLRs in all states, and the MLR was reported as a fairly coarse measure. As a result of the ACA's new Federal rule, MLRs are now adjusted for relevant factors such as insurers' size and types of products. Also, all health insurers now must consistently report their MLR and rebate data to CMS's Center for Consumer Information & Insurance Oversight (CCIIO). This agency releases to the public a detailed database about insurers' medical and non-medical expenses, and its personnel have been extremely responsive in providing information to assist our research.

The Federal MLR data source provides more transparency to consumers and permits more comprehensive and fine-grained analyses by public policy researchers. For instance, we now know for the first time how much insurers report spending on five types of quality improvement activities. And, we can analyze how different types of insurers (nonprofit, investor-owned, provider-sponsored) differ in their various financial measures.

Some analysts initially predicted that Federal regulation of MRLs would cause financial distress, perhaps severe, in the health insurance industry. To the contrary, there is no convincing evidence so far that the MLR rule has weakened the insurance industry. The individual market has become somewhat less profitable, operating at a 1 to 2 percent loss, but the group markets continue to generate operating profits in the range of 3 to 4 percent of premiums (before taxes and not considering earnings from investments and other lines of business). The industry's financial strength is confirmed by the stock market, where health insurers' stock prices have increased substantially more than marketwide averages since the ACA was enacted.[3]

Also, the MLR regulation has not caused anything like the exodus of insurers that was prophesized by some. Between 2011 and 2012, there was been a small reduction in the number of active insurers, consistent with the marketwide consolidation that was ongoing prior to the ACA. But still, throughout the country there were roughly 500 insurers with at least 1,000 members in each market segment (individual, small-group, and large-group).

Future Considerations

The ACA's MLR rule applies to commercial health insurance. A separate provision in the ACA also sets a minimum of 85 percent for private plans sold through Medicare (Medicare Advantage and Medicare Part D). There is no Federal rule, however, for the MLRs of private managed care organizations (MCOs) that provide coverage under Medicaid. About a dozen states set their own Medicaid standards, however, and others consider MLRs when they negotiate Medicaid payment rates with private managed care plans.[4]

In view of the substantial expansion of Medicaid that the Federal government is funding through the ACA, this Committee might want to consider whether the current state-based system of MLR oversight for Medicaid plans is functioning optimally. Dr. McCue and I have not done an extensive analysis of MLRs for Medicaid MCOs. However, our initial review of NAIC and other state data from 2011 indicates that, nationwide, the median MLR among Medicaid MCOs is about 87 percent.

---

[3] Pradip Sigdyal & Giovanny Moreano, Surging Health Care Index Sets Another Record, CNBC (Apr. 2, 2013), *www.cnbc.com/id/100538665;* Anna Bernasek, The Dawn Of Obamacare Hasn't Hurt Insurers' Stocks, N.Y. TIMES, Oct. 27, 2013, at BU7, *http://www.nytimes.com/2013/10/27/business/insurers-stocks-unhurt-by-the-dawn-of-obamacare.html.*

[4] Kaiser Family Foundation, Medicaid MCOs and Medical Loss Ratio (MLR) Requirements (April 2012), *http://kff.org/medicaid/fact-sheet/medicaid-mcos-and-medical-loss-ratio-mlr/.*

36

Of 211 such plans, 75 of them (35 percent) reported MLRs below 85 percent, and 30 (or 14 percent) reported MLRs below 80 percent.

In addition to bringing the bottom of this distribution up to a level considered acceptable, another potential benefit of a Federal MLR rule for Medicaid could be greater uniformity in how Medicaid MCOs measure and report their MLRs. One issue on which states vary is the extent to which Medicaid MCOs may count care management/coordination expenses as medical costs vs. administrative overhead. Also, it is not clear how states do (or should) account for Medicaid MCOs that sub-contract with other organizations or provider groups on a capitated basis. Subcapitation occurs with some frequency, but when it does, it is not clear to us whether the entire capitated amount should count as a medical expense, or instead wither the sub-contractor's own administrative expenses and profits count toward the "parent" MCO's non-medical overhead (by reducing how much of its capitation payment counts as "medical").

A Federal rule would standardize these accounting and reporting conventions. A uniform rule would also provide the opportunity for collective deliberation over which of various accounting approaches is superior. On the other hand, states vary in the extent to which their Medicaid MCO programs cover different populations with diverse health care needs, such as children, disabled adults and the elderly. Also, states differ in how they develop capitation rates for these different populations. This variation may make it more difficult to adopt a single metric that applies nationally.

Thank you for this opportunity to testify. I will be happy to answer any questions.

The CHAIRMAN. Thank you very, very much. And Senator Thune has given me permission to call—this out of order, and, therefore, I apologize, but it is worth it because it is Senator Amy Klobuchar. She wants to talk about 30 seconds. She has to go to a very important meeting.

STATEMENT OF HON. AMY KLOBUCHAR, U.S. SENATOR FROM MINNESOTA

Senator KLOBUCHAR. I just want to thank you, Mr. Chairman, for holding this hearing, and echo what Senator Thune said about your leadership and what this has meant. I can tell you in my state, we actually were an early state, a long history, as many of our witnesses know, in leading the way in healthcare, and the issue of medical loss ratio is no different.

Beginning in 1993, we required insurers to spend a minimum amount of premium dollars on healthcare and quality for consumers. I think we all know that was not happening in every State, and that is why this was so important. We basically had a patchwork system.

So far under this new rule, Minnesotans have received—people and businesses have received about $10 million in rebates. And I just want to thank you for the work on this, even for a state like ours that was ahead of our time and continues to like to see more of a focus on delivery system reform even beyond the medical loss ratio in terms of high quality, low cost care. This is a major part of it, and I want to thank you for your work.

The CHAIRMAN. Thank you, Senator Klobuchar. In honesty, I have to be fair. Senator Johnson, if you have anything. No? OK. Then Ms. Katherine Fernandez of Houston, Texas.

STATEMENT OF KATHERINE FERNANDEZ, HOUSTON, TEXAS

Ms. FERNANDEZ. Chairman Rockefeller, Ranking Member Thune, and members of the Committee, thank you for inviting me to speak today. My husband, Louis, and I have been self-employed for nearly 33 years in Houston in various aspects of residential construction.

We grew from a trim carpentry company in 1981 to a full-service remodeling company which was active until 2003. Now, we have two businesses, My Design Team which we founded in 2003 and my Cabinet Source which we founded in 2010. We have two children, Michael, aged 29, who is a grad student, and Sarah, who is 24 and a sign language interpreter.

Evaluating, qualifying for, paying for, and keeping health insurance took a lot of time because we did not qualify for group health insurance plans. I felt like I was gambling with our future. What health crisis would occur, and what could we afford to spend for insurance when there were compelling medical expenses which did not apply to our deductibles. Michael and Louis both had preexisting conditions, which meant their plans had exclusion clauses.

There were lean years in the 1990s when we had no insurance and relied on public clinics, charities, and home remedies. I was resourceful and carefully apportioned our medical spending to make every penny count. And my mom says she remembers that we just did not go to the doctor.

After that, I juggled two or three health plans at a time, balancing cost and risk. Insurance companies sent biannual notices increasing rates and offering choices of higher deductibles with reduced coverage and lower cost. Hours were spent fretting about what we could afford, and I worried about the chances we were taking. If more than one person got sick, could we pay two or three deductibles? Could we afford necessary healthcare not covered by insurance? It was like walking a tight rope with no net.

Between 2000 and 2003, we had two policies, and the insurance cost increased about 165 percent. From 2004 to 2005, despite adjusting the coverage and deductibles, the costs rose yet again over 30 percent. Mike went to college, and I bought a low cost student health insurance plan for him. In 2006, Louis stayed on our original plan, while Sarah and I moved to a less expensive one. We kept the three plans despite combined increases of 45 percent until 2009 when Mike graduated from U of H and got a Presidential fellowship for grad school at Columbia, and it included health insurance. It was a relief.

The Affordable Care Act became law in 2009, and I was elated. No more preexisting condition clauses, and we could not be dropped by insurance with no reason. No lifetime limits on coverage was great, and there would be preventative care with no co-pay. Insurance companies had to refund some of what we paid if they did not spend enough. What reasonable ideas.

In 2010, Sarah was on a student plan, and I had a low cost HSA eligible plan. Louis kept his original plan, but with an increased deductible. The cost still rose about 25 percent by the end of 2011. In 2012, I moved Louis to an HSA plan, and we upped the deductible so our coverage would cost less than before. Then the cost of my policy actually decreased in April from $316 to $310 a month. I was amazed, and I credited the ACA.

Fortunately, Sarah was still on her student plan because in April 2012 she became very sick and spent six days in the emergency room and hospital. For the first time ever, we met our insurance deductibles.

Letters from the insurance companies in July 2012 told us there would be an ACA medical loss ratio rebate for our 2011 insurance. The three checks added up to $794.82. I could hardly believe it. Our insurance cost just over $10,400 in 2011, and that refund was for 7.6 percent of the amount. I used the money to pay the next month's insurance bills.

Sarah graduated from Lamar College in May 2013 and was hired as a sign language interpreter. In July she proudly bought her own health insurance, so Louis and I were down to two HSA eligible plans. In July 2013, the insurance companies sent medical loss ratio payments for 2012. This time the three checks added up to $228.51. It was less than the next month's insurance, but was 2.6 percent of the $8,642 we spent on insurance in 2012.

Last year, our plans cost over $8,800, so I hope we will get medical loss ratio refunds again. Even more, I hope the insurance company cost estimates become more accurate so the money stays in the wallets of consumers like where it can do some good.

During the past 14 years, we have paid over $100,000 for health insurance. These were bare bone plans with high deductibles, not gold policies. Between 2000 and 2010, we spent about $72,000. If the 7.6 percent medical loss ratio refund for 2011 is an indicator, we overpaid about $5,500 during those 11 years, about $500 per year. Truly the ACA medical loss ratio provision was long overdue.

In December of this past year, I braved the health insurance marketplace and spent hours researching policies and more time trying to get the website to work. For the first time since 2005, my husband and I are on the same health plan, a silver plan PPO, and it feels pretty good.

The ACA medical loss ratio provision makes our healthcare dollars work better for us. Buying insurance is not as complicated and less of a gamble because the companies must return what they do not spend for healthcare, and basic preventative care is covered, too.

Thank you for giving me the opportunity to share my story, and I will be happy to answer any questions you might have.

[The prepared statement of Ms. Fernandez follows:]

PREPARED STATEMENT OF KATY FERNANDEZ

Chairman Rockefeller, Ranking Member Thune, and members of the Committee,

Thank you for inviting me to speak today. I am Katy Fernandez. My husband Louis and I have been self-employed for nearly 33 years in Houston in various aspects of residential construction. We started with a trim carpentry company in 1981, which grew into a full service remodeling company, which was active between 1988 and 2003. We currently own two businesses: My Design Team (founded in 2003) and My Cabinet Source (founded in 2010). Our children are Michael, age 29, a grad student; and Sarah, age 24, a sign language interpreter.

Evaluating, qualifying for, paying for, and keeping health insurance took a lot of my time since we didn't qualify for group health plans. I tried to determine the best way to handle health care for our family and felt like I was gambling with our future—how could I predict what health crises would occur, and what we could afford to spend on health insurance when there were compelling medical expenses [1] which

---

[1] Including chiropractic, acupuncture, orthopedic braces, dental care and glasses.

didn't apply to our deductibles. Michael[2] and Louis[3] both had pre-existing conditions, which meant the plans we could get had exclusion clauses.

There were lean years in the 1990s where we had no insurance and relied on public clinics, charities,[4] and home remedies. I was resourceful, and carefully apportioned our medical spending to make every penny count.

After that, I juggled two or three health plans at a time, balancing expenses and risk. Insurance companies sent biannual notices increasing rates, and offering "choices" of higher deductibles with less coverage at reduced cost. I spent hours fretting what we could afford, and worried about the chances we were taking. If more than one person got sick—could we pay two or three deductibles? Could we afford health care not covered by insurance if we were paying so much for insurance? It was like walking a tightrope with no net.

Between 2000 and 2003, we had two policies, and the insurance cost increased about 165 percent. In 2004–2005, I adjusted coverage and deductibles, yet the cost of this new arrangement rose over 30 percent during those two years. Mike went to college and I bought a student insurance plan to save a little money. In 2006, Louis stayed on the original plan, while Sarah and I moved to a lower cost one. We kept these three plans, despite combined increases of 45 percent, until 2009, when Michael graduated from UH and received a Presidential Fellowship which included health insurance at Columbia. What a relief.

The Affordable Care Act became law in 2009, and I was elated. No more pre-existing condition clauses and we couldn't be dropped by insurance for no reason. Lifting lifetime limits on coverage was great, and there would be preventative care with no copay. Insurance companies had to refund some of what we paid, if they didn't spend enough. What reasonable ideas.

In 2010, Sarah had a student plan and I had a low cost HSA eligible plan. We kept the Louis' original plan, and increased the deductible. The cost still rose about 25 percent by the end of 2011.

In 2012, I moved Louis to an HSA Plan and upped our deductibles, so our coverage cost less than before. When the cost of my policy decreased from $316 a month to $310 in April, I was amazed! I credited the ACA.

I kept Sarah on the student plan. This was fortunate, because she became very sick in April, 2012, and spent six days in the emergency room and hospital. For the first time ever, we met an insurance deductible.

In July 2012, letters came from the insurance companies notifying us of rebates required by the ACA Medical Loss Ratio for plans bought in 2011. The three checks added up to $794.82.[5] I could hardly believe it. Insurance cost just over $10,400 in 2011 and that refund was for 7.6 percent of the amount. I used the money to pay the next month's insurance bills, of $721. 83.

After Sarah graduated from Lamar College in May, 2013, she was hired as a sign language interpreter. In July, she proudly bought her own health insurance, so Louis and I were down to two HSA eligible plans.

In July, the insurance companies sent ACA Medical Loss Ratio payments for 2012. This time the three checks added up to $228.51.[6] It was less than the next month's insurance, but did amount to 2.6 percent of the $8642 we spent on insurance in 2012.

Last year, our plans cost over $8,800, so I hope we'll get Medical Loss Ratio refunds again. Even more, I hope the insurance company cost estimates become more accurate, so that more money stays in the wallets of consumers like me, where it can do some good.

---

[2] From birth, Mike had a benign muscle weakness and insurance explicitly excluded everything related to this. As a teenager, he developed scoliosis, which led to additional exclusion clauses.

[3] Louis contracted chronic Lyme disease, which was not diagnosed for many years because the various symptoms didn't look like they were related. After it was diagnosed, he couldn't change policies due to this "pre-existing condition".

[4] MDA and Shriners

[5] 2011 Rebates: Sarah's Assurant policy was $69.90, Louis' BCBS was $372.99; Katy's BCBS was $351.93.

[6] 2012 Rebates: Sarah's Assurant policy was $70.87; Louis' BCBS was $75.22; Katy's BCBS was $82.42.

I figured out that over the past fourteen years we paid for just over $100,000 for health insurance.[7] These were bare bones plans with high deductibles, not "gold"

---

[7] *Fernandez Family insurance plans, monthly payments, and price changes from 2000–2013*

August 2000–April 2001
Louis, Katy, and Sarah: BlueCross Blue Shield (BCBS) Family Plan, $252/month
Michael: BlueCross BlueShield (BCBS) Individual Plan, $39/month

May 2001–October 2001
Louis, Katy, and Sarah: BCBS Family Plan, $268/month (+$16)
Michael: BCBS Individual Plan, $42/month (+3)

November 2001–April 2002
Louis, Katy, and Sarah: BCBS Family Plan, $349/month (+$81)
Michael: BCBS Individual Plan, $55/month (+13)

May 2002–November 2002
Louis, Katy, and Sarah: BCBS Family Plan, $389/month (+$40)
Michael: BCBS Individual Plan, $61/month (+$6)

December 2002–August 2003
Louis, Katy, and Sarah: BCBS Family Plan, $499/month (+$110)
Michael: BCBS Individual Plan, $79/month (+$18)

September 2003–November 2003
Louis, Katy, and Sarah: BCBS Family Plan, $523/month (+$24)
Michael: BCBS Individual Plan, $79/month (+$0)

December 2003
Louis, Katy, and Sarah: BCBS Family Plan, $669/month (+$146)
Michael: BCBS Individual Plan, $101/month (+$22)

January 2004–July 2004
Louis, Katy, and Sarah (New Plan): BCBS Family Plan, $550/month (-$119)
Michael: BCBS Individual Plan, $101/month (+$0)

August 2004–November 2004
Louis, Katy, and Sarah: BCBS Family Plan, $550/month (+$0)
Michael: BCBS Individual Plan, $133/month (+$32)

December 2004–May 2005
Louis, Katy, and Sarah: BCBS Family Plan, $596/month (+$46)
Michael: BCBS Individual Plan, $155/month (+$22)

June 2005–July 2005
Louis, Katy, and Sarah: BCBS Family Plan, $635/month (+$39)
Michael: BCBS Individual Plan, $155/month (+$0)

Aug 2005–November 2005
Louis, Katy, and Sarah: BCBS Family Plan, $635/month (+$0)
Michael (New Plan): United American Ins. Co., $126/month (-$29)

December 2005
Louis, Katy, and Sarah: BCBS Family Plan, $721/month (+$86)
Michael: United American Ins. Co., $126/month

January 2006–June 2006
Louis (New Plan): BCBS Individual Plan $291/month
Katy and Sarah (New Plan): Unicare High Ded. Family Plan, $154/month
Michael: United American Ins. Co., $126/month (+$0)

July 2006–December 2006
Louis: BCBS Individual Plan $291/month (+$0)
Katy and Sarah: Unicare High Ded. Family Plan, $154/month (+$0)
Michael: United American Ins. Co., $143/month (+$17)

January 2007–March 2007
Louis: BCBS Individual Plan $322/month (+$31)
Katy and Sarah: Unicare High Ded. Family Plan, $161/month (+$7)
Michael: United American Ins. Co., $153/month (+$10)

April 2007–September 2007
Louis: BCBS Individual Plan $322/month (+$0)
Katy and Sarah: Unicare High Ded. Family Plan, $169/month (+$8)
Michael: United American Ins. Co., $153/month

October 2007–December 2007
Louis: BCBS Individual Plan $322/month (+$0)
Katy and Sarah: Unicare High Ded. Family Plan, $195/month (+$26)
Michael: United American Ins. Co., $153/month

January 2008–March 2008
Louis: BCBS Individual Plan $363/month (+$41)
Katy and Sarah: Unicare High Ded. Family Plan, $195/month (+$0)
Michael: United American Ins. Co., $153/month (+$0)

April 2008–August 2008
Louis: BCBS Individual Plan $363/month (+$0)
Katy and Sarah: Unicare High Ded. Family Plan, $211/month (+$16)
Michael: United American Ins. Co., $153/month

policies. Between 2000 and 2010, we spent about $72,000. If the 7.6 percent Medical Loss Ratio refund for 2011 is an indicator, we overpaid about $5,500 over those eleven years, about $500 per year. Truly, the ACA Medical Loss Ratio provision was long overdue.

In December, I braved the Health Insurance Marketplace and spent hours determining the best policy for us, and more time trying to get the website to work. For the first time, since 2005, my husband and I are on the same health plan, a Silver Plan Cigna PPO, and that feels good.

The ACA Medical Loss Ratio provision makes our health care dollars work better for us. Buying insurance is less complicated and less of a gamble because the companies must return what they don't spend for health care and basic preventative care is covered, too.

Thank you for giving me the opportunity to share my story. I'll be happy to answer any questions you might have.

The CHAIRMAN. Thank you, Ms. Fernandez. That was extraordinarily direct and sincere testimony. You could sort of feel the pain as you were talking.

Ms. FERNANDEZ. It was painful.

September 2008–November 2008
Louis: BCBS Individual Plan $363/month (+$0)
Katy and Sarah: Unicare High Ded. Family Plan, $264/month (+$53)
Michael: United American Ins. Co., $153/month (+$0)

December 2008–August 2009
Louis: BCBS Individual Plan $375/month (+$12)
Katy and Sarah: Unicare High Ded. Family Plan, $264/month (+$0)
Michael: United American Ins. Co., $153/month (+$0)

September 2009–November 2009
Louis: BCBS Individual Plan $375/month (+$0)
Katy and Sarah: Unicare High Ded. Family Plan, $324/month (+$60)

December 2009–February 2010
Louis (New Plan): BCBS Individual Plan $323/month (–$52)
Katy and Sarah (New Plan): Unicare High Ded. Family Plan, $300/month (–$24)

March 2010–November 2010
Louis: BCBS Individual Plan $323/month (+$0)
Katy (New Plan): BCBS HSA Individual Plan, $326/month
Sarah (New Plan): Assurant Student, $98/month

December 2010–February 2011
Louis: BCBS Individual Plan $360/month (+$37)
Katy: BCBS HSA Individual Plan, $344/month (+$22)
Sarah: Assurant Student, $98/month

March 2011–November 2011
Louis: BCBS Individual Plan $360/month (+$0)
Katy: BCBS HSA Individual Plan, $344/month (+$0)
Sarah: Assurant Student, $109/month (+$11)

December 2011
Louis: BCBS Individual Plan $415/month (+$55)
Katy: BCBS HSA Individual Plan, $344/month (+$0)
Sarah: Assurant Student, $109/month (+$0)

January 2012–March 2012
Louis (New Plan): BCBS HSA Individual Plan $283/month (–$132)
Katy (New Plan): BCBS HSA Individual Plan, $316/month (–$28)
Sarah: Assurant Student, $109/month

April 2012–December 2012
Louis: BCBS HSA Individual Plan $283/month (+$0)
Katy: BCBS HSA Individual Plan, $310/month (–$6)
Sarah: Assurant Student, $129/month (+$20)

January 2013–June 2013
Louis: BCBS HSA Individual Plan $298/month (+$15)
Katy: BCBS HSA Individual Plan, $312/month (+$2)
Sarah: Assurant Student, $109/month

July 2013–November 2013
Louis: BCBS HSA Individual Plan $283/month
Katy: BCBS HSA Individual Plan, $312/month

December 2013
Louis: BCBS HSA Individual Plan $362/month (+$79)
Katy: BCBS HSA Individual Plan, $343/month (+$31)
Sarah, Mike, Katy, and Louis in 2012

The CHAIRMAN. Yes. Ms. Grace-Marie Turner, President of Galen Institute. Welcome.

STATEMENT OF GRACE-MARIE TURNER, PRESIDENT, GALEN INSTITUTE

Ms. TURNER. Thank you, Chairman Rockefeller, Ranking Member Thune, Senator Johnson, for the opportunity to testify today. Not only am I President of the Galen Institute, I also served last year as a member of the Long Term Care Commission, and I want to thank you, Senator Rockefeller, and your hard-working staff. The Commission would not have been able to get started without your hard work. And I really appreciate your leadership and commitment.

And also, I want to thank you for a hearing that you participated in, I believe a Subcommittee hearing, on July 16, 2009 entitled, "Competition in the Healthcare Marketplace." It was a bipartisan hearing in which there was agreement that innovation and consumer choice are so important to those on both sides of the aisle. And I felt it was so important that the Galen Institute subsequently organized a series of annual conferences on the value of innovation in healthcare. We brought people who are doing things like creating the operating rooms of the future and developing new technologies for biomedical research to really help policymakers see the value of reinforcing innovation. And I thank you for your inspiration for that series of conferences.

So I do not think there is any disagreement that we share the goal of today's hearing on delivering better healthcare and better value to consumers. But I am concerned that some provisions of the ACA may actually be working against that goal. I explain in more detail in my written testimony, but just to highlight some key points.

First, higher taxes and fees. Higher taxes on insurance are passed along to consumers in the form of higher premiums. While it is too soon to know what the premiums will be for 2015, some consumers may experience some premium reductions, but many others are going to see premium increases. And since they were expecting a $2,500 reduction in premiums per family, even any small increase is more than they had been expecting.

The 20 new and higher taxes in the health law on things like drugs, medical devices, and health insurance are actually increasing premiums. According to the American Academy of Actuaries, they said, "In general, insurers pass along the fee to enrollees through an increase in the premium." A tax on health insurance alone will add between $350 and $400 a year to premiums in 2016 for a family. And as Senator Thune said, with nearly a trillion dollars in new taxes, ultimately they do get passed along to the consumer. I am worried that these additional costs are going to counteract any efficiencies that come from the medical loss ratio provision.

Number two, lack of competition. Premiums for health insurance vary across states as you in your work have certainly demonstrated. An article last week in the *New York Times* explains that a lack of competition is the key reason that people see such premium differences. For example, a 27-year-old enrollee in Jackson, Mississippi, may have to pay $336 a month for health insurance for a silver plan, but that same young person in Tucson only would pay $138 a month for a similar plan.

The reason, according to research that I cite in my testimony, is a lack of competition among insurers. There are only two insurers in Mississippi, but eight offering plans in Tucson. If all plans that are operating in those states were to participate in the exchanges, premiums across the board would be 11 percent lower. So competition and more participation in the market I think is crucial to getting premiums down and protecting consumers.

Third, limiting options for small employers. Small employers, many of them, have looked to health savings accounts and other consumer-directed plans to help provide health insurance to their employees, and also to help keep their costs down. As Mr. Fernandez was explaining, health savings accounts have been attractive to many small businesses. But there is a provision in the medical loss ratio regulation that actually works against HSAs. The money that a person spends on routine medical costs out of that account does not count as a medical expenditure toward the medical loss ratio provision. So they are disadvantaged in being able to use those consumer-directed accounts—money they have set aside to pay for routine medical costs. The medical loss ratio provision works against those with HSAs.

Then finally, the need for investment in a better system. In some ways, health plans actually have less incentive to seek out fraud and abuse. For example, the MLR makes it more difficult for plans to spend money on fraud detection because that spending comes out of their administrative calculation. And also, if they invest in a new delivery system but it does not fit within the very tight constraints of what is defined as quality improvement in the law, then plans are again penalized. This has the impact of impeding innovation and creativity in trying to get better value for customers.

So finally, I believe that the ACA does need to be amended and changed going forward, and I look forward to the opportunity to work with you on this common goal of producing value, innovation, and protecting consumers. Thank you, Mr. Chairman.

[The prepared statement of Ms. Turner follows:]

PREPARED STATEMENT OF GRACE-MARIE TURNER, PRESIDENT, GALEN INSTITUTE

Chairman Rockefeller, Ranking Member Thune, and members of the Committee, thank you for the opportunity to testify today on "Delivering Better Health Care Value to Consumers: The First Three Years of the Medical Loss Ratio."

My name is Grace-Marie Turner, and I am president of the Galen Institute, a non-profit research organization focusing on patient-centered health policy reform. I served as an appointee to the Medicaid Commission from 2005–2006, as a member of the Advisory Board of the Agency for Healthcare Research and Quality, and as a congressional appointee to the Long Term Care Commission in 2013.

The Long Term Care Commission, as you know, was created as a result of the repeal of the Community Living Assistance Services and Supports Act (CLASS Act), repeal legislation that Ranking Member Thune sponsored and which was enacted after the administration was unable to find a viable path forward for implementation of the program. I want to thank you, Chairman Rockefeller, for your leadership and the hard work of your staff in kick-starting the work of the commission. I believe that we produced, in our 100-day sprint to complete our work, a valuable report that gained bi-partisan support for a wide range of important recommendations.[1]

In addition, Mr. Chairman, I want to thank you for the hearing on July 16, 2009, on "Competition in the Healthcare Marketplace" before the Subcommittee on Consumer Protection, Product Safety, and Insurance which Sen. Pryor chaired and which you attended.[2] I found the hearing to be extremely valuable in showing the broad bi-partisan support for competition and innovation in the health sector. As a direct result, we have subsequently sponsored at the Galen Institute a series of major annual conferences on "The Value of Innovation in Health Care." We invite speakers from around the country to describe their work on health care innovation before policymakers in Washington, from presentations about the operating room of the future, to the latest biomedical research technologies, and transformative consumer solutions such as Walmart's $4 generic drugs program.

Consumer protections

I don't think there would be any disagreement on either side of the aisle about the goal of today's hearing, entitled "Delivering Better Health Care Value to Consumers." Consumer protection and transparency are crucial goals of health reform. To make sure that consumers can know the amount of premium dollars being spent on medical care versus administrative expenses, the ACA specifies the medical loss ratio (MLR) which health plans must meet. Plans participating in the individual and small group markets must spend at least 80 percent of premium dollars on medical costs and those in the large group market, 85 percent. Those who fail to meet the percentages must provide rebates to consumers.

Consumers and businesses already have received rebates from health insurance companies that failed to meet the MLR requirements. Certainly they appreciate receiving these checks, but I think it is important to look at the larger issue of consumer protections to see if the law is meeting these goals.

While it is too soon to know what premium increases will be in 2015, it is fairly certain that most consumers will see at least modest increases but others are likely to see significant hikes. Given that consumers were promised they would save an average of $2,500 a year on premiums for a family if the ACA were enacted, they are looking for relief. I believe it is important to look at other factors that are keeping premiums high.

Higher taxes and fees

The American Academy of Actuaries details in a May 2014 report the major drivers behind expected 2015 premium increases.[3] "The majority of premium dollars goes to medical claims, which reflect unit costs (*e.g.,* the price for a given health care service), utilization, the mix and intensity of services, and plan design." Further, the report explains, "Premiums must cover administrative costs, including those related to product development, enrollment, claims processing, and regulatory compliance. They also must cover taxes, assessments, and fees, as well as profit (or, for not-for-profit insurers, a contribution to surplus)."

The report discusses the increase in the health insurer fee, which collects about $8 billion a year from health insurers this year, increasing to $14.3 billion in 2018 and more than $100 billion over ten years.[4] "In general, insurers pass along the fee to enrollees through an increase in the premium," the actuaries write. The tax on health insurance alone will add $350 to $400 to a family's health insurance premiums in 2016.[5]

Other taxes and fees in the health law also will be passed along to consumers. These include taxes on medical devices and drugs, new fees to administer health insurance exchanges, and reinsurance fees to help offset higher-cost patients in the individual market.

These additional costs directly resulting from the law will be much larger than any health insurance efficiencies under the MLR.

Lack of competition

Premiums for health insurance vary greatly across the states. A recent report in *The New York Times* explains that lack of competition is a key reason.[6] For example, a 27 year old enrollee in Jackson, Mississippi, pays $336 a month for the second cheapest silver plan on the federally run exchange in the state. That's more than twice what the same person in Nashville would pay—$154—and more than the $138 a young person in Tucson would pay for the same policy.

A crucial reason for the price differences: Lack of competition among insurers. There are only two insurers in the market in Mississippi. In Nashville's exchange, four insurance companies compete. In Tucson, eight companies are vying for the 27 year old's business. More competition leads to lower prices.

Premiums in the exchanges are 11 percent higher than they would be if all of the insurers participating in a market in each state had participated in the exchange, according to research soon to be published by economists Leemore Dafny and Christopher Ody from Northwestern University and Jonathan Gruber of the Massachusetts Institute of Technology. Greater competition not only would save consumers money in lower premiums but it also would save taxpayers money if they didn't have to subsidize the higher cost of insurance in these areas with little competition.

When hospitals know that only a few health plans are competing, they have much less incentive to negotiate discount prices. That manifests in higher premiums because insurers can't drive as hard a bargain to reduce costs. The end result of less competition among health plans is higher costs for consumers.

I include in the appendix to my testimony a list of health insurance companies that announced they were exiting the market over a period of 20 months after the law was passed. They are leaving for a variety of reasons. Some companies decided that they could not viably compete in the exchanges, others were overburdened with onerous state regulations, and others left the health insurance market because of concerns about the ACA's costs and regulations.

Consumers need more, not less, competition, both from existing as well as new innovative companies, in order to contain premium costs.

Limiting options for small employers

The MLR rules also discriminate against high-deductible health plans, which are especially popular among small businesses with slim profit margins. These businesses want to offer health insurance to their workers but often cannot afford the generous plans that larger companies offer. Health Savings Accounts (HSAs) and other consumer-directed plans allow companies to provide an affordable alternative to their workers. HSAs provide consumers with a spending account to pay for routine health care expenses as well as good catastrophic coverage to cover major costs.

However, the MLR regulations only include in the medical cost ratio those payments made directly by insurers toward medical expenses. Health care costs paid by individuals from their spending accounts don't qualify, making it hard for these plans to meet the 80 percent MLR test. In other words, HHS rules mean that if an individual pays directly for a health care service to meet the deductible, the expenditure does not count toward the MLR ratio, even though the full amount is actually a payment for medical services.

As of January, 2013 about 15.5 million people were covered by HSA plans. The average deductible for small group HSA plans ranged from $2,820 to $2,957 in 2011, according to the latest figures available from the industry group America's Health Insurance Plans. Only about 5 percent of HSA policies have claims above the deductible.[7]

Therefore, one of the tools that small businesses have found to be most valuable in helping them offer affordable coverage is significantly constrained by the MLR rule.

Investing in a better system

Certainly consumers want to see the great majority of their premium dollars going to medical care. But the complex systems still being developed to implement the ACA require a major investment in new technology, both on the part of government and health plans.

Because of the serious problems with healthcare.gov and with many state websites, health plans received inaccurate information about enrollees and were forced to complete applications manually. This process was time consuming and extremely costly. In addition, the "back end" of the website to process information for payment is not yet built and when it is, it will require companies to build new interfaces to connect with the exchange computers—again adding to administrative cost. No one wants this, but it is a necessary investment for the system to work. There are also administrative costs associated with the detailed reporting required of the companies to comply with the MLR.

In addition, the final MLR rules released on December 2, 2011, rejected insurers' requests that the health expenditure side of the MLR equation include anti-fraud efforts. That means the new MLR rules constrain the ability of health plans to fight fraud because that spending now must count toward their administrative expenses. If health plans spend too much protecting policyholders from fraud, the plans will be penalized and forced to send rebates to the policyholders. This has the unfortunate result that health insurance companies actually have a *disincentive* to fight fraud and protect policyholders' premium dollars.

The National Association of Insurance Commissioners also had petitioned HHS to exclude broker fees from the administrative portion of the calculation. That request also was rejected by HHS regulators. This means agents and brokers, many of whom function as valued outside human resources departments for many small and medium-sized employers, will have trouble getting compensated for their work. The brokers help individuals and employers to find the policies that meet their needs, negotiate terms, benefits, and premium costs with insurers, and then help navigate the claims process for the client. With limited commissions, individuals and small businesses will not have access to these services and will have to fend for themselves.

The National Association of Insurance and Financial Advisers said it was disappointed that the final regulations did not permit insurers to exclude agent and broker fees from administrative expenses.[8]

Transparency

A shared goal of health reform is to promote transparency. Several insurers are developing a collaborative effort to provide consumers with more transparent information about prices. For example, Aetna, Humana, and UnitedHealth are working with a new nonprofit research organization called the *Health Care Cost Institute* to develop and provide consumers "free access to an online tool that will offer consumers the most comprehensive information about the price and quality of health care services." Other health plans could soon join Aetna, Humana and UnitedHealth in the effort.

Many companies also are working hard on delivery system reform and investing in initiatives to improve the quality of care, but establishing these initiatives requires an upfront investment that must come out of their administrative expense allocation, affecting their MLR calculation. The ACA regulations, however, are very restrictive in what is allowed for these developmental costs to be excluded from the MLR, and this impedes their incentive to innovate.

Given the right incentives and more flexibility to respond to consumer demands, the industry could develop new consumer-friendly initiatives to increase quality and transparency. Giving consumers more choices, transparency in costs and benefits, and the ability to select from among meaningfully different health plans are keys to developing a more responsive system.

Conclusion

While we certainly share the goal of protecting consumers to assure that they get better value in health care and health coverage, I am concerned that provisions of the ACA actually work against that goal. Higher taxes and fees on health insurance are passed along to consumers in the form of higher premiums. A lack of competition among insurers in states means there is little incentive for hospitals and other providers to negotiate lower rates, again driving up the cost of premiums. The ACA has the unintended result of interfering with one of the health insurance options that has been popular with small business by not counting spending on medical care from Health Savings Accounts as medical expenditures for purposes of the MLR calculation. And other provisions also produce unintended consequences, such as giving health insurers less incentive to fight fraud and making it more difficult for insurers and brokers to be there to assist individuals and small businesses with insurance decisions and claims.

I believe the ACA must be modified going forward. I look forward to the opportunity to work with you on the shared goal of getting consumers the best value for their health care dollars. Thank you for the opportunity to testify today, and I look forward to your questions.

APPENDIX

Health plans have left markets [9]

Health insurance carriers began leaving markets soon after the ACA was enacted. They are leaving for a variety of reasons. Some companies decided that they could not viably compete in the exchanges, others were overburdened with onerous state regulations, and others left the health insurance market because of concerns about new costs and regulations.

If there are fewer insurance companies offering coverage, consumers and employers are limited in their choices. This also means they are limited in their options to shop among competing plans to find the one that offers the best value for the best price. In addition, the insurance carriers themselves have less negotiating power with providers if there are fewer insurers in a market.

The end result is that there is less competition in the health insurance market in many states and that means higher costs for consumers.

Here is a list that we compiled in 2011 as examples of carriers leaving the private health insurance market.

In New York, Empire BlueCross BlueShield said it will drop in the spring of 2012 health insurance plans covering about 20,000 businesses in the state. Mark Wagar, president and CEO of Empire, said that the company will eliminate seven of the 13 group plans it currently offers to businesses that have two to 50 employees. The move is expected to have a great and potentially "catastrophic" impact on small businesses in New York, according to James L. Newhouse, president of Newhouse Financial and Insurance Brokers in Rye Brook, NY.[10] This loss of competition inevitably will lead to higher prices and fewer choices for businesses and their employees.

In Colorado, World Insurance Company/American Republic Insurance Company announced in October 2011 that it is leaving the individual market, citing the company's inability to comply with insurance regulations.[11] Also in Colorado, Aetna will stop selling new health insurance to small groups in the state and is moving existing clients off its plans this year, affecting 1,200 companies and 5,200 employees and their dependents.[12] Aetna also has pulled out of Colorado's individual market because of concerns about its ability to compete there, dropping 22,000 members.[13] It also has dropped out of the small-group market in Michigan and several other states.

In Indiana, nearly 10 percent of the state's health insurance carriers have withdrawn from the market because they are unable to comply with the Federal medical loss ratio requirement. Indiana was hoping to bring the companies back by asking the Department of Health and Human Services for a waiver from the rule, but Washington refused in late November 2011 to grant the waiver.

In Iowa, 13 plans have left the health insurance market since June of 2010, citing regulatory concerns.[14]

In New Mexico, four insurers—National Health Insurance, Aetna, John Alden, and Principle—stopped offering insurance to individuals or to small businesses—drying up the market and driving out competition.[15]

In Virginia, shortly after the health law was enacted in 2010, a new Virginia-based company, nHealth, announced it was closing its doors, saying that the regulatory burdens posed by the health law made it impossible to gain investor support to continue operating.[16]

The American Enterprise Group announced in October 2011 that it would stop offering non-group health insurance in more than 20 states.[17] As a result, 35,000 people will lose the health coverage they have now. The company cited regulatory burdens, including the medical loss ratio requirements, in explaining its decision to leave the markets. This means less competition in these 20 states, resulting in higher prices for consumers in many cases.

Principal Financial Group, based in Iowa, announced in 2010 that it would stop selling health insurance, impacting 840,000 people who receive their insurance through employers served by the company. The company assessed its ability to compete in the new environment created by the ACA and concluded its best course was to stop selling health insurance policies.[18]

Another 42,000 employees of small and midsize employers learned in January 2011 they were losing their health coverage with *Guardian Life Insurance Co.* of America. The company announced it was leaving the group medical insurance market (and it had reached an agreement with UnitedHealthcare to renew coverage for Guardian clients).[19] Guardian began withdrawing from the medical insurance market in specific states more than a decade ago, and says it would be leaving the market with or without the ACA.

Cigna announced that it is no longer offering health insurance coverage to small businesses in 16 states and the District of Columbia, California, Connecticut, Florida, Georgia, Hawaii, Illinois, Kansas, Missouri, New Hampshire, New York, North Carolina, Ohio, Pennsylvania, South Carolina, Texas, Virginia, and Washington, D.C.[20]

These announcements that carriers are leaving markets accelerates a trend that the American Medical Association says leaves four out of five metropolitan areas in the United States without a competitive health insurance market.[21] The report found that in about half of the metropolitan markets, at least one health insurer had a commercial market share of 50 percent or more. In 24 states, the two largest health insurers had a combined commercial market share of 70 percent or more.

This is a negative and destructive trend, leaving fewer carriers to serve these markets and giving small businesses and the insurance agents who serve them less leverage to negotiate better benefits and lower rates among competing companies.

Endnotes

[1] "Report to the Congress," Commission on Long Term Care, September 30, 2013, *http:// ltccommission.lmp01.lucidus.net/wp-content/uploads/2013/12/Commission-on-Long-Term-Care -Final-Report-9-26-13.pdf.*

[2] "Competition in the Healthcare Marketplace," Hearing before the Subcommittee on Consumer Protection, Product Safety, and Insurance of the Committee on Commerce, Science, and

Transportation, United States Senate, One Hundred Eleventh, First Session, July 16, 2009, *http://www.gpo.gov/fdsys/pkg/CHRG-111shrg54498/pdf/CHRG-111shrg54498.pdf.*

[3] "Drivers of 2015 Health Insurance Premium Changes," American Academy of Actuaries, May 2014, *http://actuary.org/files/2015_Premium_Drivers_FINAL_051414.pdf.*

[4] "PPACA Health Insurer Annual Fee Guidance Issued," Towers Watson, March 2013, *http://www.towerswatson.com/en-US/Insights/Newsletters/Americas/health-care-reform-bulletin/2013/PPACA-Health-Insurer-Annual-Fee-Guidance-Issued.*

[5] Letter from Joint Committee on Taxation to Senator Jon Kyl, June 3, 2011, *http://www.ahipcoverage.com/wp-content/uploads/2011/11/Premium-Tax-JCT-Letter-to-Kyl-060311-2.pdf.*

[6] Eduardo Porter, "One Reason Health Insurance Premiums Vary So Much," *The New York Times,* May 15, 2014, *http://www.nytimes.com/2014/05/16/upshot/why-health-insurance-premiums-vary-so-much.html.*

[7] David Hogberg, "ObamaCare Rule May Bar HSAs, Low-Cost Health Plans," *Investor's Business Daily,* December 7, 2011, *http://news.investors.com/Article/594079/201112071853/obama care-rule-hits-hsa-high-deductible-plans.htm.*

[8] "NAIFA President Robert Miller Comments on HHS Final MLR Rule," National Association of Insurance and Financial Advisors, December 2, 2011, *www.naifablog.com/2011/12/hhs-final-mlr-rule.html.*

[9] Grace-Marie Turner, "Testimony before the U.S. House of Representatives Committee on Small Business Subcommittee on Investigations, Oversight and Regulations, Hearing on New Medical Loss Ratios: Increasing Health Care Value or Just Eliminating Jobs?" December 15, 2011, *http://www.galen.org/assets/Turner_MLR_Testimony.pdf.*

[10] John Golden, "Insurer to drop small-business health plans," *Westfair Online,* November 11, 2011, *http://westfaironline.com/2011/17248-insurer-to-drop-small-business-health-plans/.*

[11] Letter from American Enterprise Group Inc. to Indiana Insurance Commissioner Steve Robertson, October 20, 2011, *http://cciio.cms.gov/programs/marketreforms/mlr/states/indiana/in_american_enterprise_letter.pdf.*

[12] Michael Booth, "Aetna to drop small groups in Colorado," *The Denver Post,* September 29, 2010, *www.denverpost.com/business/ci_16199735.*

[13] "Aetna Drops Individuals in Colorado," United Press International, February 1, 2011, *www.upi.com/Business_News/2011/02/01/Aetna-drops-individuals-in-Colorado/UPI-5825129 6591876/.*

[14] Adam Belz, "Iowa insurer exits some individual health policies," *The Des Moines Register,* October 20, 2011.

[15] Trip Jennings, "Health insurance companies drop NM policies for individuals, small groups," *The New Mexico Independent,* October 26, 2010, *http://newmexicoindependent.com/65802/health-insurance-companies-drop-nm-policies-for-individuals-small-groups.*

[16] James A. Slabaugh, nHealth letter to nHealth agents, June 2, 2010, *www.richmond bizsense.com/images/nhealthletter.pdf.*

[17] Adam Belz, "Iowa insurer exits some individual health policies," *The Des Moines Register,* October 20, 2011.

[18] Reed Abelson, "Insurer Cuts Health Plan as New Law Takes Hold," *The New York Times,* September 30, 2010, *www.nytimes.com/2010/10/01/health/policy/01insure.html.*

[19] Jerry Geisel, "Guardian to Exit Group Medical Insurance Market," *Business Insurance,* January 27, 2011, *www.businessinsurance.com/article/20110127/BENEFITS02/110129919.*

[20] Cigna Corporation, "Annual Report Pursuant to Section 13 or 15(d) of the Securities Exchange Act of 1934 for the Fiscal Year Ended December 31, 2010," *www.cigna.com/about_us/investor_relations/sec_filings/4Q2010/cigna10k20101231.html.*

[21] David W. Emmons, Ph.D., José R. Guardado, Ph.D., and Carol K. Kane, Ph.D., *Competition in Health Insurance: A Comprehensive Study of U.S. Markets, 2011 Update,* American Medical Association, *https://catalog.ama-assn.org/Catalog/product/product_detail.jsp?productId=prod 1940016.*

The CHAIRMAN. Thank you very, very much. Let me just start by asking Wendell Potter, you raised an interesting point. And if one looks across the scope of the Affordable Care Act, there are adjustments that have been made. There are adjustments that need to be made.

But I am struck by a dichotomy. On the one hand, you are saying that the medical loss ratio may have the effect of reducing the ability of insurance companies to back innovation or do innovation, whatever. And on the other hand, as Wendell has said and as I also believe, that the reception on Wall Street for insurance companies has been more positive even than it was before the medical loss ratio came in.

How does one work with those two arguments?

Mr. POTTER. Well, thank you, Senator. You are exactly correct. Since the law was passed, health insurers have done quite well financially.

The CHAIRMAN. But she is making a point, though.

Mr. POTTER. I am sorry?

The CHAIRMAN. She is saying, and you can speak for yourself, Ms. Turner, she is saying that innovation is being discouraged or potentially could be discouraged.

Mr. POTTER. But I do not think that is the case, Senator. I think innovation will continue to take place. You have to keep in mind that there is still a very competitive marketplace there, and companies have to be—— have to answer to their major customers. Most of the big insurance companies have corporate customers that demand innovation, that demand that they spend resources on fraud and abuse activities.

On that score in particular, I know that big companies in years past would spend enormous amounts of money on fraud and abuse detection technology. I remember during my years at Cigna, my staff disseminated a press release about the money that Cigna had invested with IBM on its fraud and abuse management system.

And insurers will always be spending money on that because it will be demanded by their customers that they do.

That will not go away. And much of the investment already has been made, and it is important that they continue, and they will continue that.

In other ways, their profits have continued to go up. Their revenues continue to go up partly, and, in fact, significantly, because of the Affordable Care Act they are getting more revenues that they are able to convert to profits. And they are paying their executives very generously. In fact, the CEO of Aetna, according to the proxies, just within the last few weeks was paid $30 million. The increases are continuing to go up.

Part of this can be addressed by just reallocation of some of the resources on the administrative side. When I was at Cigna, for example, we had—we spent a quarter of a million dollars for a meeting on a single day for a few hours for an investor in New York. So there is a lot of money that is not being spent prudently.

And those are premium dollars, to the money can be reallocated, as we are seeing that already happening. They are reallocating some resources. Even the for-profits are realizing that they can indeed meet the minimum standards of the medical loss ratio and operate quite well, thank you. Thank you, Senator.

The CHAIRMAN. OK. Thank you. Let me go onto Senator Thune.

Senator THUNE. Thank you, Mr. Chairman. And, Ms. Turner, in my statement, I quoted a couple of letters from constituents I had received about Obamacare. And I think, as I said, outside of Washington you hear these concerns where people are experiencing higher premiums, higher deductibles, canceled coverages, and that sort of thing, which is, I think, compounded by an expectation that there were going to be lower premiums in many cases.

And I am wondering maybe if you could share your thoughts about those price increases, and perhaps put into perspective whether or not the benefit that they derive from the MLR provision is exceeded by the cost of these other increases that are occurring with regard to deductibles, and premiums, and that sort of thing. Could you put that into context?

Ms. TURNER. Well, thank you, Senator. I have an example in my testimony about the health insurance tax costing the average family $350 to $400 a year. I do worry that that one tax alone counteracts much more than the savings that a family might get from their—that most families would receive from their medical loss ratio rebates.

But there are so many other provisions in the law that are driving up the costs of premiums. I think all of us have been hearing many complaints from consumers about the fact that the mandated benefits package is so rich. Yes, we never know what health crisis we are going to face, but many people feel that the benefits that they are paying are far outside what they need and would use. And they also feel that the deductibles are too high. Also having preventative care be a so-called "free benefit" means that the cost of that care must be built into the premium itself.

So there are a lot of provisions of this law that keep consumers from being able to make their own choices about what kind of health insurance policy works for them and what kind of policy they can afford. And I also believe that if consumers had more choices in a less-constrained market, that would put pressure on the insurance industry to make sure that they do provide value.

Senator THUNE. Professor Hall, there is a lot of interest in Congress in preventing fraud in Medicare and Medicaid. And the government is seeking to move beyond what is referred to as pay-and-chase model of recouping fraudulent claims after the fact. In fact, our colleague, Senator Nelson, just introduced a bipartisan bill to improve Medicare's fraud prevention.

And the question I have with regard to that as it pertains to the MLR rules, which allow fraud recovery expenses to be treated as medical claims, so there is effectively a disincentive for insurers to invest in fraud prevention activities, which concerns me as some fraud obviously affects patient care.

So could you discuss how the current rule helps or hurts fraud prevention?

Mr. HALL. Excellent question, Senator. I have not studied the nuances of that in great detail. I do know that the general spending on fraud is only a fraction of a percent, so whatever effect the rule has, the fraud issue is just a very small sliver of the total pie.

I do believe that the issue was given very thorough consideration, not only by HHS, but also by NAIC. And with a lot of these sort of issues of definition and line drawing that had to be confronted, I think one thing the rule brought to light was just good data about what is happening, and a really sort of thoughtful consideration from all viewpoints as to what the best resolution would be.

So I do not if it is the perfect resolution, but I do think that the issue is, as you noted, to treat fraud recovery in a more favorable way, but perhaps fraud investigation as an administrative cost is— I do not know if it is a compromise, but it says there is a line and we define what is on which side of the line.

And within that, there is broad leeway for insurers to do what they think is best in their best interests and their policyholders' interests. To say that you can spend 15 or 20 percent of the premium dollars on administrative costs leaves an awful lot of room to decide how much of that should go toward sales, toward profits, and toward fraud recovery.

Senator THUNE. Ms. Turner, would you want to add anything to that? It seems, to me at least, it is better to stop fraud when it occurs rather than to attempt to recoup money that has already been appropriately paid. I mean, does that not ultimately benefit patients?

Ms. TURNER. Absolutely. And I think that when you do look at the incentives, if a company is paying out a dollar that is not actually for legitimate medical care, if it just pays the dollar, then it counts as a medical expenditure even it is not appropriate. But if they go after the dollar and try to get it back, then the cost of detecting the inappropriate billing counts against their administrative expenses. So I do think that the incentives really do work at cross purposes.

And one of the things that really constrains companies is figuring out how to do this juggling act with all of the other costs of regulatory compliance, taxes, setting up networks, and getting physicians and hospitals enrolled in their plans. They just may not have the investment capacity as Mr. Potter indicated they did before the medical loss rule went into effect.

Senator THUNE. Mr. Chairman, my time is up.

The CHAIRMAN. Thank you very much. Senator Johnson?

STATEMENT OF HON. RON JOHNSON, U.S. SENATOR FROM WISCONSIN

Senator JOHNSON. Thank you, Mr. Chairman. Yes, I will be the first to admit here that almost everything here in government is well intentioned, but there are some very serious negative unintended consequences.

According to the Manhattan Institute for Policy Research, in the State of Wisconsin, a 27-year-old male after the Affordable Care Act, their premiums now are 124 percent higher than they were than pre-patient protection Affordable Care Act. A 27-year-old female is experiencing 77.6 percent higher premiums. So that is certainly part of the collateral damage that we are seeing as I am getting e-mails, as Senator Thune talked about.

Just a couple of quotes from real people telling the truth, not telling lies. "You need to understand how cheated we feel. This is not right. I cannot afford this." By the way, that individual's premium went from $550 per month to almost $1,600 per month. "Please help. Sir, I'm begging for your help. I'm very feeling very upset and stressed." That came from a couple with cancer. "The law is hurting us. Be our voice. I guess we are collateral damage. We are scared."

These are statements from e-mails, hundreds that we have received from real Americans, from real Wisconsinites. And I realize there are plenty of people who are also being advantaged by the Affordable Care Act, but it is because their care is being subsidized either through higher premiums or direct subsidies from government that are going to be paid for our kids and grandkids because, you know, we are still running deficits.

Mr. Potter, you used the word "excess profits." Can you define "excess profits?" What is an acceptable level of profit in a commercial enterprise?

Mr. POTTER. I do not think there is an acceptable level of profits. I think it depends on what your—you might have an opinion and——

Senator JOHNSON. Well, do you think profit is OK because, I mean—do you expect people to engage in commercial activity? Do you expect people to put their capital at risk and not ever have any chance for making a profit?

Mr. POTTER. Well, Senator, keep in mind in this country we still have many, many non-profit health insurance companies. We did for many years, and they worked quite well. And so, there are some companies that have decided that they want to be in this business to make money. That is their ultimate objective. Then you have another insurance companies that that is not their sole objective.

Senator JOHNSON. I understand, but you actually have a concept that somebody can make too much money, but you are not willing to say what that would be.

Mr. POTTER. Sir, I do not think that is what I intended to say at all.

Senator JOHNSON. There is a chart on page 11 of the majority report, a study apparently done by the Health—what is it, the American Health Insurance Plans. And apparently this was a group that tried to quantify how much money was spent and in what areas of healthcare. Apparently it was inaccurate it seems like from the majority's standpoint. But what they showed was about a 3 percent profit rate. Was that pretty much your experience when you were working in the healthcare industry?

Mr. POTTER. No. You can get that number when you add in the non-profit health insurance companies to the equation. And I know America's Health Insurance Plans quite well from having been in the industry for quite a long time.

Senator JOHNSON. So I am asking you, what would be the average profit rate for a for-profit insurance company?

Mr. POTTER. It varies. It can be five, six, seven percent, and that could be significant. You could also look at the return on equity, which is also pretty high. But let me look at it from this perspective.

Senator JOHNSON. I just want to try and drill down some numbers. So you are talking after-tax profit rate somewhere, five, six, 7 percent, and you are probably thinking that is excessive.

Mr. POTTER. I think it is pretty significant. You have to keep in mind what these companies have done in the past to make sure that they are earning that. They refuse to——

Senator JOHNSON. I am running out of time. I need to go to——

The CHAIRMAN. I will give you more time, but let him answer the question.

Senator JOHNSON. You will give me more time?

Mr. POTTER. Yes, for many years, insurance companies engaged in practices that enabled them make whatever profits they made, such as refusing to sell coverage to people at all because of pre-existing conditions who are charging them so much that they could not afford to buy coverage.

It is why, Senator, we had about 50 million people who could not get coverage. And, yes, there are some people now who are probably paying more for their coverage, but before the Affordable Care Act, there were many millions more who could not afford coverage.

Senator JOHNSON. You are not—again, I have a line of questioning, and you are not answering the question. I want to go to, I guess it was Professor Hall. I think you said that the rebates totaled $1.6 billion?

Mr. HALL. Yes, Senator.

Senator JOHNSON. Ms. Turner you were talking about that the fees, the insurance fees totaled $8 billion to $14 billion.

Ms. TURNER. We are focused here today on the medical loss ratio. But the average consumers are not looking at this law in a silo. They are looking at their overall cost experience. And if their premiums are going up because of so many other provisions of the law, then their own experience is that their health insurance is costing them a lot more.

Senator JOHNSON. Yes. I just want to bring that into perspective. So rebates are $1.6 billion, but the government is collecting $8 to $14 billion from those exact same insurance companies.

Ms. TURNER. In the same year.

Mr. POTTER. Do we have the same timeframe?

Ms. TURNER. Yes. Well, it is basically—it is about $8 billion, I think, in the first year for the health insurance tax alone. That does not count the medical device tax, or the drug tax, or others that I did not quantify in my testimony. But, yes, just that one tax is several times more than the medical loss ratio savings.

Senator JOHNSON. If you could indulge me one further question. I come from the private sector, so I actually have a great deal of respect for the power and quite actually the brutality of financial competition. And from my standpoint, in running a business, an after-tax profit of five percent is not particularly a really high profit business.

So my question is, if these are excess profits or we have not delivered good value to customers, where is the breakdown in the marketplace? Why is that? Because truthfully when you have a lot of competitors, they are fighting for business, and with a 5 percent after-tax profit rate, that to me seems like there is a fair amount of competition. So where was the breakdown? Could it be because we had state markets and limited competition between States? What drove that?

Ms. TURNER. Are you asking me, Senator?

Senator JOHNSON. Sorry. Whoever would like to answer, I am fine with that.

Ms. TURNER. Absolutely. State regulation has really impeded competition, and, in fact, has driven out many companies. I have a list in my testimony of companies across the country that basically have left the health insurance market, and a lot of them have left because the rules and regulations are becoming so onerous. Many are moving into other types of insurance and are leaving the health insurance business altogether.

So it is rules and regulation. It is the lack of competition. It is the difficulty and the expense of putting together networks to make sure that plans can provide services and that people have access to physicians and hospitals, all while still trying to keep their premiums low. It's very difficult.

Mr. HALL. And if I could give my response as well, I think with respect to competition and this rule, I think it is a more nuanced story in a sense that for the most part, the 80/20 rule confirmed what the markets were giving us. It pretty much was set according to the prevailing medical loss ratios, and that is why there has not been a major dislocation. To the extent that if some companies were below that level, perhaps there just was not good information or there were pockets of the market that were not as competitive as they could be.

With respect to profits, you know, typically you think five percent is an OK profit, but you have to understand that a lot of what the premium is, is giving money to the insurers that they then pay back to my doctors. And so, if you pay 5 percent to your bank to hold your money and give it back to you later or to your mutual fund, you would say that was outrageous. So I am not saying the insurance company is the same as that, but it is somewhat different than selling, you know, a commodity that has to be manufactured with a lot of risk. It falls somewhere in between.

And so, the general consensus is a two to three percent profit is sufficient to be financially healthy in the insurance industry.

The CHAIRMAN. Thank you, Senator. Senator Scott?

STATEMENT OF HON. TIM SCOTT, U.S. SENATOR FROM SOUTH CAROLINA

Senator SCOTT. Thank you, sir. I would say to Mr. Hall's comments and directly to Senator Johnson's comments, it questions the whole notion of trying to figure out how much profit is enough profit, and for someone to say they can tell you what it is, they cannot, number one. Number two, having spent a couple of years in the insurance industry on the property and casualty side, the reality of it is that the two, or three, or four, or five, or six, or seven percent profit that you see can be eliminated by any catastrophic occurrence that occurs.

The challenge with health insurance is a little different than the property and casualty business because the reality of it is that based on the adverse risk selection, you find yourselves in harm's way. And so, I think we have learned, and what we will continue to learn over the next several years, is a new definition of "adverse risk selection." And companies are going to have to adjust their premiums in order to satisfy this thirst for us to have mandatory health insurance on everyone.

Said differently, the unintended consequences are that you will see that your premiums are increasing, your deductibles are increasing, your out-of-pocket expenses are increasing. The only things that are not really increasing are the number of doctors in your network. So if you are looking for in-network doctors consistently throughout the exchanges, you will find that there are fewer, not more. If you are looking for hospitals to go to, fewer, not more.

So the real challenge is if you have a specialist or a need for a specialist, visit some of the cancer centers and see which ones are in and which ones are out. Look at the teaching hospitals and see which ones are in, see which ones are out.

The other aspect that I would suggest is that when you look at the premiums paid versus the claims paid, the real benefit for the insurance industry has been their ability to create a return on the investment based on how they use those premiums before they pay them out. So ultimately, the actual profit is generated by equity position and other assets that provides real opportunity for them to continue to provide the coverages that are necessary for us to see people insured.

Mr. Potter suggested that there were 45 or 50 million Americans who did not have health insurance because they were unable to get it because of preexisting conditions and other areas as—other issues as well. The fact of the matter unfortunately is by the year 2024, according to the non-partisan CBO—we like to call it non-partisan when we like what they have to say, although I think they lean a little left—suggests that we will see 31 million Americans still without insurance.

So what we have said is that we are going to spend between $1.5 trillion to upwards of $2 trillion to provide health insurance to about 10 or 12 more million Americans at a cost that is a couple of trillion dollars higher and perhaps destroy the best delivery system of health insurance we have ever seen in the world.

With that said, having sold health insurance back in the 90s before I woke up and realized, hey, I can do something else besides this because this is getting complicated. Now I thank God that I had the good fortune to get into the property and casualty business because people who have to do this for a living every day with this new MLR are being run out of business. And what I mean by that, Ms. Turner, is that agents are no longer en vogue.

So we have consumers making decisions on their own or with the help of a navigator. Now, I am sure that a navigator, being defined as 40 hours of good training, perhaps knows a little bit about health insurance, but not much more than the consumer. And that is one of the great challenges that we face.

So the MLR's unintended consequence is the elimination of a professional that comes into your house, sits down with your family, understands your health situation and challenges, and makes good decisions with you. That is unfortunately being eliminated every single day going forward.

I would suggest that what Mr. Thune has said previously and what I am receiving from my constituents, Mr. Turner, some of my constituents from Clover, South Carolina are seeing their premiums go from $330 a month to $525 a month.

I do like the notion that we are going to celebrate the concept of a rebate. This rebate comes in the form of cash coming home until they realize that even if they applied their rebate to their higher premiums, the rebates pales in comparison to what they had before there was a concept called the MLR, which is unfortunate.

I just cannot figure out how we justify these higher rates by suggesting that we have more people insured. It is just inconsistent with the facts that we will see play out, I believe, overall. We may see more people with an insurance card, *i.e.,* having access to health insurance or health care. But when the capacity because of the doctors and the hospitals and the specialists are being constricted, the definition of access may have to change.

So I am seeing my time is running out because the lights are changing colors, but let me ask Ms. Turner one question. It seems to me that an insurer may actually have a perverse incentive to get an MLR rate that is acceptable, but may drive costs later. So my question is this. It seems to me that an insurer who has actually some success in bending the cost curve in the delivery system of medical care will have a greater challenge in meeting their MLR. If an insurer manages to spend less on medical care through negotiating better rates with providers, that would be exactly what we want, of course. But at that point, the ratio of medical expenses to the company's fixed administrative costs is suddenly off. So it seems that the MLR actually rewards less efficient delivery of medical care. Thoughts?

Ms. TURNER. That is absolutely right. And, of course, the converse is true as well. If a company winds up paying moure out in medical costs, that means their base can be higher for their medical loss ratio administrative calculation. But the consumer is certainly disadvantaged. So absolutely, Senator.

And to your other points, emergency room physicians recently released a report saying that they are seeing a dramatic increase in the number of people showing up for care at hospital emergency rooms even though the Affordable Care Act was designed to make sure people did not have to go to emergency rooms, especially for routine care.

And to your point about agents, the agents and brokers really are like external H.R. departments for many small businesses.

Senator SCOTT. Absolutely.

Ms. TURNER. And they are enormously beneficial, not only in helping people and business owners wade through the complexities of finding the right policies, but also in helping them when they have claims and when they have challenges. And it is really, I think, very detrimental to consumers when agents are not available to help them and to help small business owners who now have to navigate this complex space on their own.

Senator SCOTT. Thank you, ma'am. Thank you, Mr. Chairman.

The CHAIRMAN. Thank you, Senator Scott. There is sort of a fascination to me of the rhythms of discussing the Affordable Care Act. First of all, if you call it the "Affordable Care Act," that means you must be an optimist with no moorings. On the other hand, if you call it Obamacare, you are just a good, solid American citizen who does not like the President or whatever.

But you see it time and time again when new legislation is introduced, and particularly when it is far reaching beyond the medical loss ratio, but the whole medical loss ratio and the whole Affordable Care Act. That, you know, a while ago everybody was spending all of their time on the computer system, which was all botched up, and that seems to have gotten better. You do not hear very much about that.

So then, and this is typical in so much legislation, that if something is working, and is settled law, and is accepted by the Nation, and people are signing up, and the exchanges are, you know, in Oregon not working quite so well, but they are going to go to the Federal model, are working, and people can stay on their parents' until they are 26 years old, and getting rid of lifetime limits, annual limits. I mean, you do not hear Ms. Turner discussing that kind of thing or Senator Johnson discussing that kind of thing because that does not fit a mindset.

But it is the old business of if you want to nail something, you read a couple of e-mails that you have gotten.

And I have never used that technique, but I do remember the e-mails and conversations and situations that I was involved in before the Affordable Care Act was passed and before medical loss ratio was passed, and there were tragedies.

I mean, I remember—Ms. Turner, this may not move you, but it moved me—a 10-year-old boy who had cancer in Charleston, West Virginia, and he was dying from that cancer. And I met with him and his family, and his annual limits, which then existed, had run out. And he had—they had spent a million dollars, and there was nothing more that would be allowed to be spent.

And that does not exist anymore. All kinds of—preexisting conditions was huge. Huge. And you refer to costs going up, and Senator Johnson refers to costs going up, and then I am thinking about what I am reading in the newspapers and reading in professional papers is that overall the cost of healthcare is going down. Now, at some point, if the cost of healthcare is going down, but the costs are going up to individuals broadly on such a scale, then the first could not possibly be true.

So again, it is the question of if you want to pierce something or to put in a bad light, pull out an e-mail or use some example because you may be—that e-mail is probably correct. It is from a real person expressing, you know, real frustrations. But again, I go back to my world, which is not as wealthy as Wisconsin, but southern West Virginia or West Virginia as a whole, and I look at Ms. Fernandez there and listening to her story. And that is what I have heard. That is what I have heard. I mean, I did not get into the business of—and Al Franken actually helped on this a lot.

I did not get into the business of the medical loss ratio, you know, which was sort of everybody was excited about the public option, and Wendell and I have discussed this before. The public option was a terrific idea, I guess, but the point is we could not get any votes for it in the Finance Committee. So you can keep on saying, like all the TV reporters did, this is a terrific idea, and the press was saying, and if you are not for medical—for the public option, you cannot be serious about healthcare reform. Well, that might have been true except the fact we could not get any votes for it to get it out of the Finance Committee much less get it on the floor of the Senate.

So then we came to the medical loss ratio, which seemed to make sense, and on a bipartisan basis was passed. And I think it is very important to take a long view at what is going on here, and I will be able to dig up some e-mails that make part of the Affordable Care Act that does not look good, especially from people who have their mind that they do not want it to work because they do not like the President. Maybe he is the wrong color, something of that sort. I have seen a lot of that, and I know a lot of that to be true.

It is not something you are meant to talk about in public, but it is something I am talking about in public because that is very true.

People associate a piece of legislation. Their leader in the Senate has committed at the beginning of the President's term to block every piece of legislation that the President puts forward. And they have done that with this exception and a few other exceptions. And I find that—I find that disingenuous behavior.

So, Mr. Potter, if the insurance company—I mean, maybe the ideas are mixed on what are excessive profits, but if, as you and Mr. Hall said, if there are profits, and if people are signing up now in very exciting numbers, and if the polls show that people overwhelmingly want this healthcare system to work as opposed to the last healthcare system. I mean, if we wanted to have a discussion about the last healthcare system, we would be here for 4 hours listening to me.

But, you know, it is a—the prospect of finding something that works for people where they have choice, where they have—make their own decisions, there are going to be—there will be some consequences. I mean, in some cases there will be fewer doctors and that is why there is a lot of money in the Affordable Care Act to specifically encourage primary care doctors to get into the business. That is why I think there is $10 billion in the Affordable Care Act to open up a thousand more rural health clinics so that people in rural areas can get to rural health clinics.

I mean, to me the concept of trying to nickel and dime and use convenient political arguments against a very, very major piece of legislation, which happily is working and will be working better all the time to the extent that in 10 years Ms. Turner is going to be telling herself, why was I complaining? Why was I complaining? It did not seem good at the time, but it seems everywhere I look people are getting satisfied.

Will we make more tweaks to the law? Will Sylvia Mathews Burwell, if confirmed by the Senate, will she continue to make some more tweaks? She will have to because anything this big has to be tweaked because there always improvements that can be made. But to me, the basic factor—I have obviously run over my time—no, actually my time setter who works for me has just suddenly I have 2 minutes and 50 seconds, Senator Johnson. It is good to be Chair.

Senator JOHNSON. You are the Chairman.

The CHAIRMAN. That is it is working and if rather than waiting for the clouds to deliver thunderbolts of lightning and doom and misery, actually things are seeming to be turning around, then realistically you do not ask for perfection on every day in every way. You assume there are some consequences. There will be some irregularities. Things will vary from state to state, and you will always begin to come up with examples.

I mean, this example of waste, fraud, and abuse I have heard on every single subject that has ever existed. And the fact is, as Mr. Hall said, I think it is actually less than one-half of 1 percent.

And that is pretty amazing. So I would just raise a protest in the way in America that we approach problems. If something is done by the other side, so to speak, then attack, attack. Do not think about what Ms. Fernandez has been through. And I am saying do think about what Ms. Fernandez has been through, and that is the point. That is why a bill had to be changed. That is why the existing healthcare system where insurance companies were making off like bandits and cutting people off——

The whole concept of rescission. I do not know if Ms. Turner knows what rescission means, but it is where somebody is paying their premiums and they have a disease which the insurance company decides is going to be very expensive. And so, the law says no more rescission. End of rescission, and that is absolutely fantastic news for hundreds of thousands of people. But you do not hear that talked about that very much because the word "rescission" is not understood very much. But I daresay that Mr. Fernandez understands it real well, and I daresay that Mr. Ralston understands it.

So again, it is the question of when you approach major legislation that affects people's lives, is it important to be fair, and is it important to—for me to understand that everything that is not working as well as it should, but it is a good bill, and it is working, and people are signing on very fast. And, you know, West Virginia amazed me by instead of going to 133 percent of Medicaid expansion went to 138 percent. And then I looked at—I am going to sign a letter with some other Senators to all the Governors who refuse to get Medicaid into the Medicaid expansion because I think it is unconscionable.

I have not heard any talk about that around here. I mean, in Texas I think it is several million people are without health insurance because of that fact. Well, why do I not hear about that? That is what Medicaid expansion is for, and all that means is that 20 Governors have to change their minds and stiffen their political spines, and do what is right. Virginia struggling is struggling with now. We will see what happens on that.

But I do think that when you are dealing with major legislation, it is important to be fair, and it is important to see the bad and the good, to balance them, and to decide whether you are going to try to move this cart forward or you are going to try and stop it. And I am not favor of trying to stop it. Nobody is going to stop it. It is the law, and it will work.

I do not think that was a question, but I enjoyed myself. But do you understand that, Wendell?

Mr. POTTER. I do, Senator.

The CHAIRMAN. It is so frustrating. When you live through what healthcare was in southern West Virginia and all of West Virginia, what people did not have, people were terrified of going to a doctor. People could not get to a doctor. And when I went to West Virginia as a Vista volunteer as an untrained social worker in 1964, it was only because there was a rural healthcare facility right across the stream in another county that we could go to. And, yes, there were plenty of people in the waiting room then, and there are more people now. And part of the reason is because people want healthcare. When people want healthcare, that is a good sign. It means they are going to be aggressive about it and look to exchanges and have a positive attitude, which I think is what pulls us through in America. Anybody want to respond to that?

Mr. POTTER. Senator, if I might start, I think—I appreciate what you were saying because so often we have lost sight of what the world was like before the passage of the Affordable Care Act and why we needed to have it in the first place. We forget that between 1998 and 2008, the average premium for a family went up 131 percent, and deductibles were going up as well, too. And the percentage of the premium that workers were paying was increasing as well, too. That is not a statistic that is cited very often these days. But we have forgotten what it was like and why so many people were priced out of the market before the Affordable Care Act.

Since my testimony 5 years ago, I was inundated with phone calls and e-mails from people who thought that I might be able to help them deal with problems with their insurance companies. And until the law was passed, there was really nothing that I could do. I could not help people get coverage if they had had a preexisting condition. I could not help people who were deemed uninsurable until the law passed.

And as you may know, Senator, one of the reasons that I decided to do what I did was going to a health fair not too far from West Virginia in Wise County, Virginia. I was down there to visit family. And I went to this healthcare exposition that was being held at a county fairgrounds, and I saw people who could have been my relatives, who could have been people I grew up with, could have been me if my circumstances had not been slightly different.

And they were standing in these long, long lines waiting to get care that was being provided, Senator, in barns and animal stalls by doctors and nurses who were volunteering their time. And it was just stunning to me.

I realize at that moment that what I was doing for a career was making it necessary for people that I could have grown up with and could have been related to get care that way. That is what had happened. That is what had happened to our so-called healthcare system. And that was just one community.

And the people who were putting that exposition together, they call them expositions, have been doing this all over the country because it is not just a problem in Wise County, Virginia. It is everywhere in this country. I left my job because I could not, in good conscience, continue doing that.

And, Senator, also insurance companies make a lot of money. They really do. And when you are talking about percentages, it may seem to be relatively small. But just the five largest health insurers last year made about $12 billion profits, just five companies. We have got about 1,300 insurance companies. They make a ton of money.

The taxes on—the so-called new tax on insurers, they do not have to pass that along. They have a lot of resources. They do not have to. They just decided they want to do that, and they can do that. They conceivably could absorb those and still make considerable money.

Also they are getting a lot of new customers. There was no incentive before the Affordable Care Act for these companies to reform this system themselves. It had to be from the outside. We have seen that for many years because of the way their practices were going, they were excluding more and more people. And we had an aging population. We were going to see more and more people falling into the ranks of the uninsured because of preexisting conditions. They do not have to pass that along.

And also, underwriting costs. They do not have to spend as much money on some things that they spent enormous amounts of money on in the past, such as underwriting that can be reallocated to and are being reallocated in certain ways to make sure that premiums are reasonable.

I have talked to many people, Senator, who have told me that their premiums are much less. And a lot of people, in fact, a majority of people who are buying coverage through the exchanges are paying less than they thought they would. They are getting subsidies that are helping them. So a lot of people are better off. Some people have told me, Senator, that they are alive today and they are confident of it because of the Affordable Care Act, and I believe it.

The CHAIRMAN. Senator Johnson, do you want to close her out here?

Senator JOHNSON. Oh, I absolutely do, Mr. Chairman. It was regrettable, and I would say it was offensive—seeing as I am the only one in the room really talking about opposition, that you would play the race card, that you would say opposition to Obamacare necessarily must stream from some inherent racism. Very offensive.

But listen, my opposition to my healthcare has nothing to do with the race of President Obama. My opposition to this healthcare law, by the way, which was passed on a 100 percent totally partisan basis. You talk about a major piece of legislation. The way it used to work in this country is something this major would normally be done in a bipartisan fashion where you would actually accommodate the other person's views. That is not what happened with this law.

The CHAIRMAN. Senator, there was no accommodation? There was no accommodation?

Senator JOHNSON. It was passed on a purely partisan basis. But my objection to the healthcare law is, first of all, if you do not know my story, my daughter was saved by this healthcare system that was supposedly so terrible. My daughter was born with a congenital heart defect. Her aorta and pulmonary artery were reversed, first day of life. One of those greedy doctors that President Obama said would take out a set of tonsils or cutoff a foot because of the fee schedule, came in at 1:30 in the morning and saved her life. Eight months later when her heart was the size of a small plum and after 7 hours of open heart surgery, a team of dedicated professionals in a fabulous healthcare system that we have rebaffled the upper chamber of her heart. She's now 31 years old. Now, she's a nurse practitioner.

The reason my story has a happy ending is because my wife and I had the freedom, and that is the problem with Obamacare. It is the greatest assault on our freedom in my lifetime. We had the freedom to call up Boston Children's and Chicago Children's. And by the way, we just had a standard healthcare plan. I had the same healthcare that every one of the people that worked with me had. Nothing special about it. We were able to access those miracles because of our healthcare system.

And we did not have to totally remake America's healthcare system to take care and provide the social safety net that we all agree on. I agree with President Obama, no American should go bankrupt because they get ill, but we did not have to pass this monstrosity. We could have done it using high risk pools. Now, in the State of Wisconsin, those are obsolete. They are gone. The couple with cancer I was talking about, they could afford their high risk pool insurance. Not anymore. They lost it. It is gone because of Obamacare.

So sure, there are some people that have been advantaged by Obamacare. I admitted that. But they are advantaged by it because taxpayers are subsidizing them. And by the way, not really taxpayers. The debt on our kids and grandkids will pay for those subsidies. Or they are being subsidized by 27-year-old men and women in Wisconsin who are paying 124 percent higher premiums. That is why some people are advantaged because somebody else is being disadvantaged.

I objected to Obamacare because of the loss of freedom. I objected to it because I understand that when you actually pay for it by reducing payments to providers, you are going to have fewer providers. You are going to have less access.

You will have rationing. The medical device tax, what has that resulted in? We are not really investing in developing medical devices for manufacturers anymore because it is too expensive. A 2.3 percent tax on gross sales, those companies are moving overseas. They will stop innovating. We will not see the types of miracles that we could have had if we had not destroyed that type of innovation.

So I did not object to this because of the race of the President. I objected to this because it is an assault on our freedom. And, Mr. Chairman, I have to admit, I have a great deal of respect for you, but I am the only one in the room, and I found it very offensive that you would basically imply that I am a racist because I opposed this healthcare law. That is outrageous.

And again, there are so many problems with—Ms. Turner, I actually have a question for you because Senator Scott brought it up. I have heard, and I do not have it—I am not going to quote a figure because I get *PolitiFact* checked all the time. I have heard of an alarming number of insurance agents that will lose their jobs because of this. Have you heard—do you know of any studies about that?

Ms. TURNER. I do not believe there have been any studies yet, but in California, for example, there have some reports in the *Los Angeles Times* and elsewhere about how hard agents worked to help enroll people in the coverage, and yet it is questionable whether or not they are going to be able to be paid. And many of them, their office costs are fixed, too. They may wind up not being able to continue to support these new enrolees.

And I do want to echo what you said about the overall goal of the law. Senator I believe in the goals of getting coverage to everybody and protecting freedom in this wonderful society we live is an absolutely important goal. But the question is, how do we do it?

Senator JOHNSON. And let me just conclude on how this thing was sold to the American people. It was a consumer fraud, a massive consumer fraud. This President looked at the American people and told them a boldfaced lie. If you like your health plan, you can keep it, period. If you like your doctor, you can keep it, period. Because of this wonderful law, the average cost of a family plan was supposed to decline by $2,500. It hasn't. It has increased by $2,500.

So the e-mails I am getting, and by the way, they are not, as Senator Harry Reid said, coming from a bunch of liars. These are coming from real Wisconsinites. They are writing about 150 to one. Yes, we are getting e-mails from people that have been advantaged by Obamacare. But 150 for every one that has been advantaged has been disadvantaged, and those are real people, and those are real stories.

So again, thank you, Mr. Chairman.

The CHAIRMAN. I can only conclude that what you in your heart deeply want for the American people is to go back to the healthcare system that we had and to have a totally free enterprise, let the insurance——

Senator JOHNSON. No, you are assuming the wrong thing, Mr. Chairman.

The CHAIRMAN. Well, I am saying——

Senator JOHNSON. You have implied that I am a racist.

The CHAIRMAN. I have not implied that you are a racist.

Senator JOHNSON. Now, you are saying you want me to go back to a failed healthcare system. You are just incorrect.

The CHAIRMAN. That is very, very silly on your part. You are evidently satisfied with a lot of people not having health insurance so long as you——

Senator JOHNSON. I am not. Quit making those assumptions. Quit saying I am satisfied with that. I am not. There was another way of doing this. I am happy to discuss it with you. I would have been happy to engage in the debate and pass a good healthcare law. As a matter of fact, I am the one pushing a bill, If You Like Your Healthcare Plan, You Can Keep It Act. I do not have any Democratic sponsors on that.

I am also working with Republican colleagues on Preserving Freedom of Choice in Healthcare to preserve freedom of choice in healthcare. What a concept, huh? So, no, please do not assume— do not make implications of what I am thinking and what I would really support. You have no idea.

The CHAIRMAN. I actually do, and, you know, God help you.

Senator JOHNSON. No, Senator, God help you for implying I am a racist because I opposed this healthcare——

The CHAIRMAN. I did not imply that you are a racist.

Senator JOHNSON. Let us play back the tape.

The CHAIRMAN. We can do that, but we are not going to. You have lost temper. I understand that.

Senator JOHNSON. I was called a racist. I think most people would——

The CHAIRMAN. You were not called a racist.

Senator JOHNSON. I would think most people would lose their temper, Mr. Chairman.

The CHAIRMAN. You were not called a racist. However, you have done everything you can to block progress. The law is the law. Every Republican voted against it against one or two. I think—did Olympia Snowe vote for it? She wanted to, but I think she was told that if she did she would lose her position on the Commerce Committee, so she did not.

It is a very partisan thing, and I regret that, but that is what the Republicans have decided to do, to block everything the President puts forward. And that is not very helpful to America.

I want to thank all four of you for your patience in listening to strong feelings, and what was important is that you had strong feelings. And I am particularly looking at you, Ms. Fernandez, because I think you are a classic story and a classic case. And you are not involved in all the folderol that we have gotten involved in here.

Ms. FERNANDEZ. May I say something?

The CHAIRMAN. Please.

Ms. FERNANDEZ. Rationing was there before. My healthcare and my family's healthcare has been rationed from the moment my son was born with a preexisting condition. There has not been freedom of choice for our healthcare because not all policies were available to us. Once my son was diagnosed, or not actually diagnosed. They just said he has got some sort of condition, the healthcare policies we were eligible for or we could find that covered him, specifically excluded all muscular and skeletal issues.

That is not health insurance. There is no way that is health insurance. If he broke a leg, it would not have been covered. It is ridiculous to talk about health insurance only from the perspective of health insurance company profits. People do not buy health insurance in order to ensure that health insurance companies get huge profits. They buy health insurance to help them cover their medical expenses, both expected and unexpected.

That is not a minor thing. It is a major thing. And people who like the Affordable Care Act often call it Obamacare because it is kind of a friendly sounding name, too. So it is not just pejorative. It is often affirming, and I think that is important.

The problem with health insurance the way it has been is that it was purely a gamble, and it was rigged. And I am tired of a rigged system. I am tired of money being made, huge profits off of misfortune, and that is what this has been for me. My family has struggled for years to try to make sure that we are all taken care of, and I have avoided having necessary medical testing purely because the cost of it was too high, and it would not be covered for health insurance. And also, I was terrified that if something was found, that my insurance was dropped. The whole system was rigged.

When you are self-employed, when your insurance is bought on the individual market, the whole system was flawed, and deeply flawed. I think the Affordable Care Act is a step in the right direction. I do not think it goes far enough to protect consumers, but I think it is way better than the system we had before. And I am not an insurance person. I am not somebody who studies things from all sorts of different perspectives how profits should be or anything like that. I am a person. I am a family member. I am a business owner. I am somebody who has tried for years to navigate a system, and this was before the Affordable Care Act, that simply did not work. And it did not work for a lot of people.

So thank you for letting me speak.

The CHAIRMAN. Sort of a good place to declare the hearing adjourned. Thank you for that.

[Whereupon, at 4:32 p.m., the hearing was adjourned.]

APPENDIX

The following two articles were submitted for the record by Senator Thune:

WHISTLEBLOWER: ACA CONTRACTOR IN WENTZVILLE PAYS EMPLOYEES TO DO NOTHING

by KMOV.com Staff

KMOV.com

Posted on May 12, 2014 at 10:44 PM

Updated Thursday, May 15 at 1:13 PM

(KMOV.com)—Employees at an Affordable Care Act processing center in Wentzville with a contract worth $1.2 billion are getting paid to do nothing but sit at their computers, a whistleblower tells News 4.

The facility is operated by Serco, which is owned by a British company awarded $1.2 billion partially to hire workers to handle paper applications for coverage under the new healthcare law.

A worker tells News 4 weeks can pass without employees receiving even a single application to process. Employees reportedly spend their days staring at their computers.

"They're told to sit at their computers and hit the refresh button every 10 minutes, no more than every 10 minutes," the employee said. "They're monitored, to hopefully look for an application."

The Centers for Medicaid and Medicare services told News 4 in a statement that "Serco is committed to making sure Federal funds are spent appropriately, and the number of Serco staff is reviewed on a regular basis."

Politico—May 11, 2014 07:04 AM EDT

$474M FOR 4 FAILED OBAMACARE EXCHANGES

By: Jennifer Haberkorn and Kyle Cheney

Nearly half a billion dollars in Federal money has been spent developing four state Obamacare exchanges that are now in shambles—and the final price tag for salvaging them may go sharply higher.

Each of the states—Massachusetts, Oregon, Nevada and Maryland—embraced Obamacare, and each underperformed. All have come under scathing criticism and now face months of uncertainty as they rush to rebuild their systems or transition to the Federal exchange.

The Federal Government is caught between writing still more exorbitant checks to give them a second chance at creating viable exchanges of their own or, for a lesser although not inexpensive sum, adding still more states to *HealthCare.gov*. The Federal system is already serving 36 states, far more than originally anticipated.

As for the contractors involved, which have borne most of the blame for the exchange debacles, a few continue to insist that fixes are possible. Others are braced for possible legal action or waiting to hear if now-tainted contracts will be terminated.

The $474 million spent by these four states includes the cost that officials have publicly detailed to date. It climbs further if states like Minnesota and Hawaii, which have suffered similarly dysfunctional exchanges, are added.

Their totals are just a fraction of the $4.698 billion that the nonpartisan Kaiser Family Foundation calculates the Federal government has approved for states since 2011 to help them determine whether to create their own exchanges and to assist in doing so. Still, the amount of money that now appears wasted is prompting calls for far greater accountability.

(67)

Where has that funding left the four most troubled states?

Nevada, for one, is still trying to figure out its future. Oregon has decided to switch to *HealthCare.gov.* Maryland wants to fix its own exchange, maybe by incorporating what worked in Connecticut. Massachusetts actually wants to do both—build a portal from scratch while planning a move to the Federal exchange as a backup.

Massachusetts' dual-track approach could require more than $120 million on top of the $170 million it already has been awarded. That cost is nearly twice as much as if the state were to simply bail on its Connector, but officials seem to be banking in part on the Obama administration's greater interest in helping the Massachusetts exchange—the once-pioneering model for Obamacare—survive.

Josh Archambault, a senior fellow with the right-leaning Foundation for Government Accountability, argued that the state's efforts to salvage its exchange are just a face-saving exercise.

"Instead of a quixotic sprint to rebuild the whole site in five months, state officials should instead pivot quickly to utilize the Federal exchange, saving taxpayers tens of millions of dollars in the process," he said.

State officials have warned that most of what is left of their initial Federal award may be needed to end their contract with CGI, the vendor that built the Connector. They acknowledged Thursday they have no guarantees of additional Federal funding.

"You have two choices," Rep. Stephen Lynch (D–Mass.) said last week. "One is to expend even greater amounts of money on something that had limited success thus far or going to the Federal exchange. . . . There's simplicity in that, and I think that may be where some within the commonwealth would like to go."

By contrast, Oregon has already opted to give up on its website and use *HealthCare.gov.* The colossal failure of Cover Oregon—which so far has cost $248 million in Federal money—has prompted a probe by the General Accountability Office. The state's congressional delegation is taking keen interest.

"The next step is the Federal investigation . . . and I'm anxious to get those results," said Democratic Sen. Ron Wyden.

But Democratic Rep. Peter DeFazio has also called for litigation against Oracle, the vendor that was supposed to set up the site. What it has been paid is "ill-gotten gain on the part of Oracle, and we should sue to get the taxpayer money back," DeFazio said Thursday.

Only 14 states and the District of Columbia developed their own health insurance exchanges for individuals to buy coverage under Obamacare, a far different scenario than the law's authors envisioned.

Nevada, the only Republican-led state to run an individual exchange this year, expects to decide on the future of its struggling Nevada Health Link in the next several weeks. An outside report concluded that salvaging the major flaws in the exchange would be a huge feat. The system has spent $51 million of the approximately $90 million in Federal grants that were authorized, according to a spokesman.

"The report seems overwhelming to me," Lynn Etkins, Vice Chairwoman of the Health Link board, said last week. "And I really am not hearing anything that all of these issues are going to be resolved well before open enrollment so testing can be done."

Senate Majority Leader Harry Reid blames Xerox, which constructed the exchange, for the many problems his state's system has had. "They're the ones that should be held accountable," he said Tuesday.

The company, however, maintains that a fix is possible. "While the list may, in fact, look daunting . . . when you get under the covers and start to look at the outputs in terms of the progress that we've made over the last several months, I am actually less daunted," David Hamilton, a Xerox official working with the state, told Etkins and other board members at their recent meeting.

Maryland is a state that aspired to be another national model but ended up spending $118 million in Federal funds on a fatally crippled exchange. It is in the process of trying to transition to the technology used by Connecticut's system. It's still unclear whether the move will meet Federal approval. If not, Maryland would default to *HealthCare.gov.*

"There's got to be oversight on how public monies are spent," said Sen. Ben Cardin (D–Md.). "But I'm not trying to say who is responsible yet. I've heard the state many times talk about the private contractors—so they've got to be part of the mix."

Rep. John Delaney (D–Md.) is a strong supporter of Obamacare but has been calling on the state to go to the Federal exchange since December. He says the move to the Connecticut exchange is a "political cover-up" and charges that officials have not been transparent about Maryland Health Connection or its repairs.

"If you stumble, you have a particular obligation to be upfront," Delaney said.

○